Your Church Has Personality

Creative Leadership Series

Assimilating New Members, Lyle E. Schaller
Beginning a New Pastorate, Robert G. Kemper
The Care and Feeding of Volunteers, Douglas W. Johnson
Creative Stewardship, Richard B. Cunningham
Time Management, Speed B. Leas
Your Church Can Be Healthy, C. Peter Wagner
Leading Churches Through Change, Douglas Alan Walrath
Building an Effective Youth Ministry, Glenn E. Ludwig
Preaching and Worship in the Small Church,
William Willimon and Robert L. Wilson
Church Growth, Donald McGavran and George G. Hunter III
The Pastor's Wife Today, Donna Sinclair
The Small Town Church, Peter J. Surrey
Strengthening the Adult Sunday School Class, Dick Murray
Church Advertising, Steve Dunkin
Women as Pastors, edited by Lyle E. Schaller
Leadership and Conflict, Speed B. Leas
Church Finance in a Complex Economy, Manfred Holck, Jr.
The Tithe, Douglas W. Johnson
Surviving Difficult Church Members, Robert D. Dale
Your Chuch Has Personality, Kent R. Hunter

Your Church Has Personality

Kent R. Hunter

Creative Leadership Series
Lyle E. Schaller, Editor

Abingdon Press / Nashville

YOUR CHURCH HAS PERSONALITY

Library of Congress Cataloging in Publication Data

HUNTER, KENT R., 1947–
Your church has personality.
(Creative leadership series)
Bibliography: p.
1. Church growth. 2. Christian leadership.
I. Title. II. Series.
BV652.25.H875 1985 254′.5 84-14596

ISBN 0-687-46875-2

MANUFACTURED BY THE PARTHENON PRESS AT
NASHVILLE, TENNESSEE, UNITED STATES OF AMERICA

Dedicated to Janet

Foreword

Sooner or later most Protestant congregations face three questions. The first concerns the definition of "our parish"—"who we are." For centuries people thought in geographic terms. They socialized with their neighbors and, if they went to church, worshiped with a congregation that met in a nearby building. That world still exists for some people, but for a decreasing number. Today the lives of most people on the North American continent no longer can be described in geographic terms.

That change has forced the leaders of many churches to begin to formulate a new definition of identity, purpose, and role. This book is intended to help congregational leaders accomplish that task. Its author, one of the foremost authorities on church growth, contends that each congregation has its own distinctive personality and that its personality, not its geographic location, is the best beginning point for planning an expansion of ministry. This volume both explains the concept and provides the tools to help leaders formulate a philosophy of ministry and put that philosophy to work.

A second question frequently arises: "Instead of placing so much emphasis on numerical growth, why don't we first focus on the personal and spiritual growth of our members and the health of our congregation?" In this book Kent Hunter makes clear that this is a simplistic misunderstanding of church growth; that all three facets of growth—the individual growth of each member, the health of the corporate community, and the outreach to the unchurched—are inseparably linked.

The third issue may be stated in these terms: "We want to begin to plan for the future of our congregation, but we don't know where to begin." Huner urges us to think in terms of the distinctive personality of each congregation. This helps us understand ourselves and also helps us affirm the rich diversity of churches in our community. Instead of seeing competitors lurking in every religious structure, an emphasis on the unique personality of each church will help us recognize that through diversity we can reach and serve more people.

This is one of a half-dozen volumes in the Creative Leadership Series that have been designed to help thoughtful congregational leaders grapple with questions of identity, purpose, role, outreach, and ministry. Those seeking additional resources may want to turn to the books by Douglas Johnson, C. Peter Wagner, Douglas Alan Walrath, Donald McGavran and George Hunter, Peter Surrey, and Steve Dunkin for further reading.

Lyle E. Schaller
Yokefellow Institute
Richmond, Indiana

Contents

Preface

At the very center of the Church Growth Movement lies the key to its effectiveness—an attitude toward comprehensive growth of God's kingdom. By *comprehensive,* I mean internal growth at the personal level and at the level of the local congregation. I also mean external growth—in the congregation's own backyard and across the face of the globe.

This attitude toward growth represents the Church Growth Movement's greatest challenge—without it, people will not be motivated for the expansion of the Kingdom. For maintenance-oriented, nominal Christians who are not attuned to growth, this change in attitude is crucial. It is essential. It also is difficult. A church growth-oriented philosophy of ministry is a tool that can help. This book is written to help God's people discover the personality, the image—the philosophy of ministry—of the Body of Christ to which they belong; it then moves on to define ways in which that particular philosophy of ministry can be intentionally permeated with New Testament principles of church growth.

In 1955, Donald McGavran published *The Bridges of God* and launched the modern Church Growth Movement. Since then hundreds of books have been published, clergy and lay people have been trained, periodicals have been born, and consultants have emerged—all committed to helping local churches fulfill the Great Commission.

Church growth is simultaneously a science and a theological stance. As a theological position, church growth is committed to the effective implementation of the Lord's Great Commission (Matt. 28:19-20). The church was established on this earth to grow. The Church Growth Movement sees a static church as unhealthy because it is unbiblical. The church as the people of God, the bride of Christ, the living building and the Body of Christ, is a living organism. The nature of a living organism is that it grows. Therefore much emphasis is placed upon evangelism and outreach. Yet growth is not emphasized in terms of quantity only. On the contrary, *quality* growth is one of the basic concerns of the Church Growth Movement. The importance of making disciples impels church growth people to stress more than just bringing people to Christ. The goal of evangelism is not accomplished until a person becomes a responsible member of the Body of Christ. As a theology for the church, church growth is comprehensive. It is an invigorating movement within the contemporary church.

As a science, church growth is pragmatic—it is concerned with putting theology into practice. Therefore it emphasizes the need to measure, analyze, plan, develop strategies, and set goals. Recognizing the great blessings of God in recent social-science advances, church growth people tap the resources of sociology, psychology, and anthropology at any time these insights can be used for the growth of God's kingdom. The resources of communication theory and management principles are also employed, as are all other means that will allow God to use his people for his eternal principles. Of course, practice never supersedes theology. Response to God's grace in Jesus Christ and submission to Scripture—these are the basics upon which the Church Growth Movement is built.

Dozens of books about the movement *briefly* mention the importance of a philosophy of ministry. This book will concentrate upon that critical and basic topic and, indeed, can be used effectively in developing a church growth philosophy of ministry. Discussion questions are located at the end of each chapter for use by groups of lay people in the implementation of that process.

As you can see, the book is designed not only for information, but as a "how to" guide as well. It can also be a useful reference tool for pastors and students of church growth as it seeks to raise readers' consciousness in the whole area of recognizing philosophies of ministry. The ultimate goal for this volume is the growth of the church, the effective implementation of our Lord's Great Commission.

I am grateful to those who helped in various ways as the manuscript was prepared; to those who reviewed and gave constructive comments—especially John and Gloria Reed, John Hitzeroth, Joann Grepke, and Don Wagner; and to those who stood by me in personal support. Most of all, I am indebted to my wife, Janet, who labored through the typing of the manuscript and encouraged and guided my work every step of the way.

Kent R. Hunter
Corunna, Indiana

I

Unity in Diversity

A sense of excitement intensified as we drove toward a suburb of Fort Wayne. The church we were to visit was well known in the northeastern corner of Indiana. We had heard that Oak Lawn Church was growing like wildfire. Almost everyone with whom we talked had seen the pastor on the church's television program, aired every week throughout the region.

As we traveled the silent Sunday-morning streets, we wondered whether anyone was reaching out with the gospel in the sprouting suburbs of this spreading city. But suddenly the deserted streets were teeming with activity. Cars turned. People darted across. Buses discharged crowds. Would we have to walk far? We weren't running *that* late!

To our amazement, there were numerous parking spots near the front door! Only later did we discover that our good fortune was planned. Toward the end of the service the pastor announced, "Once again we want to remind all our members to park in the lots across the road and down the street. Buses will pick you up and return you to your cars as usual. Remember, God has placed us here to reach this community for Christ. Parking spaces near the door are reserved for visitors."

As we entered the building our eyes were immediately

drawn to a large hanging sign: Visitors' Center. Like most visitors, we inched forward apprehensively. But our discomfort was eased when a warm welcome was extended by several people standing by a table under the sign. We were asked to fill out visitors' cards, received information about the congregation, and had name tags pinned on us.

A friendly guide led us to the sanctuary through several halls and many turns. We passed one classroom after another and finally realized we were in a school. The sanctuary was the gymnasium. We marveled at how artistically this congregation had transformed a gym into a reverent house of worship. The padded chairs, the carpets, and the platform were all moveable. The church operates a school during the week and uses the gym for sports.

During the service, several television cameras beamed the gospel beyond the four walls. We heard announcements about the evangelism program and read about the outreach ministry. As we left, we had to work our way through a hall jammed with people waiting to attend the next service.

On a cold and wintry morning, we drove past Philadelphia row houses to Saint Mark's Church in the inner city. As we approached the stately structure, people were just beginning to congregate by the large wooden front doors. The neighborhood had grown old. The residents had grown poorer. The crime rate was climbing. Amused, I wondered whether the tall fence around the church was to keep people out or hold them in.

Those black people of the congregation who had moved to other areas as their incomes grew were now commuting to their old neighborhood. A magnetism, perhaps emanating from their elderly pastor, drew them back each Sunday.

"This great big structure is a millstone around our necks," said the pastor as we strolled dark and dingy halls. "It's too much." Some pastors would give anything for these facilities, I thought. Maybe in a different location. Maybe with different leaders. Maybe with other programs.

The worship service rang with the joy of traditional hymns. I wondered whether these black people found meaning in the traditional German liturgy. The choir sang a gospel song with gusto. The Spirit of Christ was present.

As the people filed out the door, I watched and listened. The pastor knew his people by their first and last names. He stopped each one to ask a personal question. "Is your husband still ailing?" "How are the new twins?" "What about Uncle Fredrick, is he back from his visit down South?" What a warm and close-knit church, just like a family! Everybody cares. Everybody loves everybody. Each Sunday is a family reunion.

We first heard about the Fulton Free Church in a seminar on church growth. It was located in a suburb of Los Angeles. Immediately, we noticed a parking problem: It was necessary to walk a long distance to the church. No one seemed to mind.

It was some time before the first service would begin, but a long line of people was moving slowly through the front door. Most of them were young, and many were carrying Bibles and note pads. The scene gave the appearance of a college campus with students bound for a lecture.

We were fortunate to find seats, since the church was not large. Before the service began, there were wall-to-wall people—in the aisles and on the floor in front and in back. The sheer numbers caused an air of electric anticipation. By the time the pastor entered, all sensed something very special was about to happen.

We sang a hymn and joined in prayer before the sermon. Following the sheets that had been passed out at the door, the pastor led an intensive study of several verses of Scripture, with biblical exposition and practical application. Fifty minutes later the sermon ended. The plate was passed, a hymn sung, a prayer said. Church was over.

The Same, But Different

Each of these churches is a Christian church. Each confesses Jesus Christ as Savior and Lord. They are of different denominations, but is that what makes them so greatly different? They are miles apart and in various types of communities. Each has a different pastor. Each has a different group of worshipers and a different church structure. Are these what make each church different?

The answer, of course, is Yes! Every church is the same, but different. This should not be seen as a problem, but as the beauty of the Christian faith. Frequently Christians spend so much time in their own congregation that they don't really have an opportunity to discover what other congregations are like. They assume all congregations are about the same—especially those within the same denomination. This assumption leads to an attitude that considers other Christian churches competitive. Hostility develops between sister congregations.

One pastor pointed out that five churches had been built on the same major street, all within five miles of one another on Detroit's east side. He called it church row and was disgusted that the denomination would allow such terrible planning.

Actually, there was no competition. Each congregation had somewhat different priorities. One operated an elementary school and emphasized Christian education. Another conducted a strong singles ministry and stressed fellowship. Still another was characterized by a high view of liturgy and traditional services. A fourth concentrated on service to the whole person, organizing programs to meet the needs of the people in the community.

The point is that churches can exist right across the street from each other and not be a threat to the ministry and growth of either. Even congregations of the same denomination will take on different postures. Does this mean that the Christian church becomes whatever suits the whim of the people? Not at all. There is a unity within the Christian church. But inside that unity there is freedom for the individual congregation to fulfill God's plan in ways that are different. The programs, the strategies, the expression in worship, the ministries, and the buildings—all will take individual and unique shapes. But each remains within the context of the Christian faith, and each different shape constitutes a philosophy of ministry (see Figure 1).

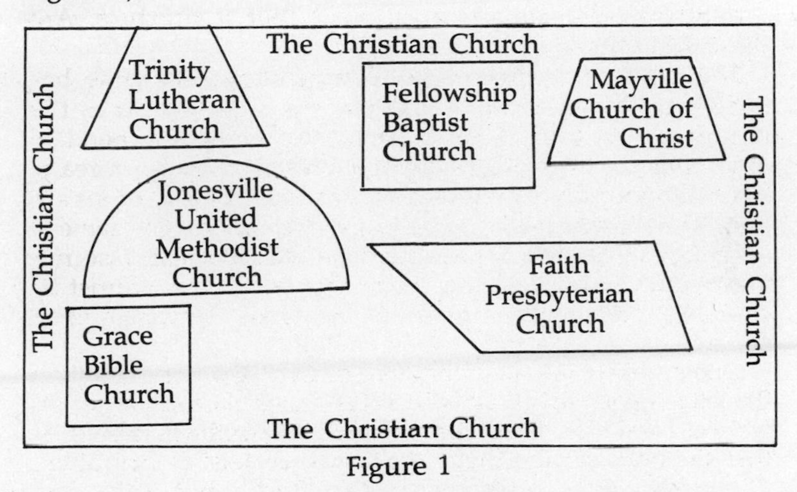

Figure 1

The Body of Christ

The Scriptures reveal various symbols to help the Christian understand the nature of the church (six of these symbols are discussed in chapter 5). The apostle Paul frequently speaks of the church as the Body of Christ. This symbol of the church as a body demonstrates that God intends the church to be simultaneously unified and diverse. This is demonstrated on several levels.

Level One

Each congregation is unified. Paul says, "For just as the body is one and has many members, and all the members of the body, though many, are one body, so it is with Christ" (I Cor. 12:12). But Paul goes on to say that within the body there is diversity. There were Jews and Gentiles within the early Corinthian church. There were slaves as well as free people. However, stressing unity again, he reminds us that all were baptized into one Body by the same Spirit (I Cor. 12:13).

Paul points out the diversity of the body in another way—through its spiritual gifts. In Ephesians (4:11ff.), for example, he tells us that each person is given a gift or gifts from God. He writes about this also in chapter 12 of the Letter to the Romans. Each person in the Body of Christ is to function according to his or her gifts. Church members are like parts of the human body. All do not act as hands or feet; there are various functions—all divinely appointed. When the members work together, using their spiritual gifts, the whole Body is built up in love.

Again, while pointing out the beautiful diversity of the Body of Christ, Paul calls attention to its unity: "There is one body and one Spirit, just as you were called to the one hope that belongs to your call, one Lord, one faith, one baptism, one God and Father of us all, who is above all and through all and in all" (Eph. 4:4-6).

Level Two

This same unity and diversity can be seen in a given community. The New Testament talks about "the church in Jerusalem" (Acts 11:22, e.g.). The modern reader probably thinks of a single structure on the corner of two busy streets, with a sign out front giving the topic of next Sunday's sermon. In fact, "the church" in Jerusalem was undoubtedly a large number of house churches. Early Christians frequently worshiped in their homes. This was the case not only in Jerusalem but probably in other New Testament churches such as those in Ephesus and Corinth and in the region of Galatia.

The apostles had no problem in seeing the church as unified, even though it was geographically diverse. They correctly understood the church as a living organism. The church was diverse but unified because the church was the "called out" people of God.

Level Three

The Christian Church is seen as universal. It includes those of various cultures and in various distant regions (I Cor. 1:2). The unity of the church is not bound by locality, language, or worship style. On all three levels, the church is both unified and diverse (see Figure 2).

Beautiful Diversity

In this so-called ecumenical age it is not very popular to praise God for diversity. Yet as the church expresses itself in programs, life-styles, and worship forms, there is a stroke of genius for which Christians can be thankful. Churches differ because people are different.

The Body of Christ

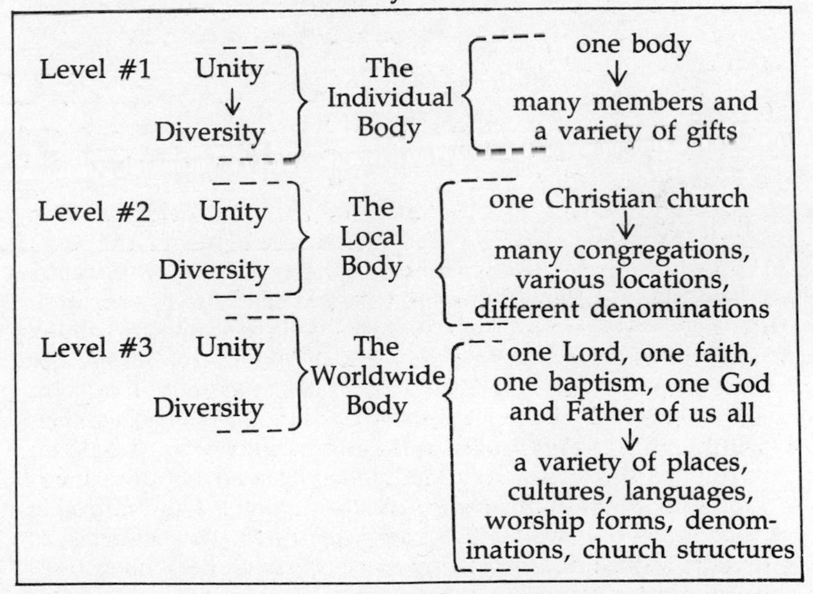

Figure 2

Your Church Has Personality

Different people are attracted to different churches. A man who loves music and attends the symphony every week may not feel at home in a storefront church with no music. The person who did not finish the eighth grade may not be comfortable as part of the classroom-type church where the pastor lectures and the people take notes. As long as there is a variety of people who need to be won to Christ, the people of God will praise him for a variety of churches.

This does not mean that congregations should not cooperate. When an evangelistic crusade is being held, for example, congregations can join for common goals of publicity or busing. When a hunger drive is conducted for starving refugees, churches from diverse backgrounds can cooperate in gathering food. The point is that congregations from various backgrounds share a common task; they do not share a common life-style.

All true Christian churches share a common Savior. They do not necessarily share the same style of worship. All truly Christian congregations confess one Lord, one faith, one baptism. They do not necessarily have the same priorities.

Each church operates with a different philosophy of ministry. This does not deny the unity of the Body of Christ. Rather, it gives witness to the diversity of God's creation. He is a God of variety. His people reflect that variety.

The problem is that most congregations do not know they are unique. Worse, they don't know why. They don't understand what it is that makes them special. They have never consciously spelled out their philosophy of ministry. There is no intentionality about why they do what they do.

Congregations that wish to be healthy and churches that desire to grow should set out to discover their philosophy of ministry and intentionally change or direct that philosophy toward good sound goals of growth. As stewards of God's many resources, Christians can use their philosophy of ministry to promote the optimum growth of God's kingdom in many ways.

Discussion Questions for Chapter I

1. What principles (not programs) of a philosophy of ministry can you detect in each of the three churches mentioned at the beginning of Chapter 1?
   (a) Oak Lawn Church, Indiana: ____________________

   ____

   ____

   ____

   (b) Saint Mark's Church, Pennsylvania: ______________

   ____

   ____

   ____

   (c) Fulton Free Church, California: __________________

   ____

   ____

   ____

2. What principles (not programs) of a philosophy of ministry can you detect in your own congregation?

   ____

   ____

   ____

   ____

3. With what other congregations in your geographic area are you familiar? List them and determine in what ways they are different from or the same as your congregation.

Congregation	Different	Same
______________	______________	______________
______________	______________	______________
______________	______________	______________

4. Make a list of the people in your discussion group. In what ways are you all the same? In what ways are you different? Do you know your spiritual gifts? How does your group express the unity and diversity of God's people?

____

____

____

____

5. Have you ever thought of your congregation as unique? In what ways—for purposes of church growth—does your church capitalize on its uniqueness? List ways it could promote its uniqueness for growth to glorify God.

____

____

____

____

II

What Is Your Philosophy of Ministry?

When asked about his congregation's philosophy of ministry, one pastor said, "We just preach and teach the Bible." That sounds like a nice pious answer and, in a way, should be true of all Christian churches. But it isn't useful for describing what makes a church unique.

So I asked again, "What is it that makes your church unique?" He really hadn't thought about it, he said. So I asked the question another way: "What is important to you here—something that other churches in the area might not stress as much as you do?"

"Oh, why didn't you say so?" he replied. "We have the best youth program in town. We have a gymnasium. We provide roller skating every week. We have drama clubs and run a coffee house on the weekends. . . ." That was part of the answer. There was more.

"What do you require for membership?" I asked.

"We don't have a lot of rules and regulations. We live by the love of the gospel."

"When someone joins your church, what do you tell them the people of *this* church do? Do you expect them to attend worship?"

"Of course!" he said. That was another part of the answer.

"Do you expect or encourage all people to be in a Bible study or join a fellowship group or give offerings regularly by a percentage?" I asked. Now he was beginning to see that his church had a peculiar identity. It was a unique living organism. It had an ecclesiastical personality!

An Ecclesiastical Personality

Every congregation has a personality. Whether written or not, each church has a philosophy of ministry. There are many factors that make up such a philosophy. A church may even have some characteristics that are totally opposite from the philosophy the people are trying to promote.

People who want their church to grow should realize that communication is both verbal and nonverbal. There is a story about a man who worked in a factory. Each day he left carrying a box. To make sure no one stole anything from the factory, the security guard would check the workers as they left. Each day the man would carry out the box, and each day the security guard would check the box to be sure it was empty. The reality was, of course, that the man was stealing boxes!

Communication theory tells us that often the medium is the message. In other words, a church may have a relevant, up-to-date gospel to preach. But because the church looks old and run down, those who have never heard the gospel may receive a message that will keep them from ever getting close to it. Communication can be both verbal and nonverbal.

This is one problem a church faces in a changing community. A white neighborhood may turn black. The church is still white and the members commute. The congregation may indeed want to reach out to the black newcomers to the area. But the blacks look the situation over from a distance and see only whites attending the church. They conclude, wrongly, that blacks would not be welcomed. Or if they do attend, what do they see?—white ushers, white preachers, white choir members, and white worshipers. That's why it often takes a long time for a blood transfusion to take place in the Body of Christ in a changing community. A philosophy of ministry is demonstrated in many ways, regardless of what we preach.

How the Church Spends Its Time, Energy, and Money

One congregation called itself a mission church, dedicated to the Great Commission. But after a study determined the amount of *time* spent on certain priorities, a different reality emerged. The study was easy to conduct. One member was appointed to be an observer at all board and committee meetings during a particular month. This member sat quietly, but monitored the time spent on maintenance-related items as opposed to mission-related items. It was discovered that most of the meeting time was devoted to maintenance goals: How do we keep the institution running?

When a church is interested in growth, every board and committee will be involved in outreach and expansion. Even the board of trustees will be outreach-oriented. Trustees with church-growth eyes will continually monitor the building's appearance as if they were new prospects attending for the first time. And, mundane but mission-related: Can the visitor find the bathroom? Church-growth sensitive people will take steps to see that visitors are comfortable. They want them to come back again . . . and again.

Trustees should always envision future growth. Where can the church expand? Land adjacent to the church lot has become available for purchase—how can it be financed? Is there a long-range goal to plant a church in another community? If so, how do they fund it? These may be matters for trustees, but they are also important mission matters. Every church board and committee should spend a major portion of its time on growth goals and strategies.

The way the church spends its *energy* is another good test of its philosophy of ministry. A survey at Calvary Church asked every active person to calculate how much time each spent in church work during a certain month and to estimate the percentage of time involved inside and outside the church for outreach. Results revealed that most time dedicated to the work of the Lord tended toward projects *inside* the church.

Upon further investigation it was discovered that much of what went on at Calvary could be described as fellowship. Fellowship is good, and it is a vital part of a healthy church. But when a church has too much fellowship at the expense of church growth, the church is sick. In C. Peter Wagner's *Your Church Can Be Healthy*, he describes this disease as koinonitus, an infection of fellowship that causes spiritual navel gazing.[1] A congregation's philosophy of ministry is partially demonstrated by the way the people spend their energy.

Donald McGavran has analyzed *five classes of church leaders* (see Figure 3).[2] For a church growth philosophy of ministry, a good balance of workers must be represented. *Class one leaders* are volunteers who work within the church. *Class two leaders* are also volunteers, but they work outside the church to help bring in new members. *Class three leaders* are partially paid and are usually found in smaller churches. *Class four leaders* are full-time, paid professional staff. *Class five leaders* are denomination executives or regional bishops. The healthy, active, growing church will have many workers involved within the congregation, but about 20 percent of those volunteers will be doing work that reaches out.

The philosophy of ministry of a congregation also is characterized by the way it spends its *money*. Our Redeemer Church discovered that about 50 percent of its budget supports a parochial day school. Obviously, the school is a top priority. The congregations's philosophy may be based strongly on education.

A Healthy, Growing Congregation

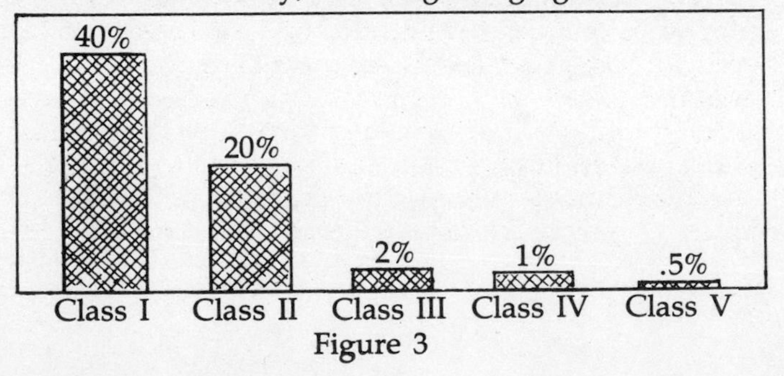

Figure 3

Economics is a strong determinant in the church. People spend their money on items that are important to them. Often people do not "put their money where their mouths are." No matter what they say, the way they spend their money reflects their true priorities. The budget is a good indication of a congregation's philosophy of ministry.

The Church Constitution

Many churches have a constitution based on the goal that everything "should be done decently and in order" (I Cor. 14:40). Church growth says that this premise is *not* the purpose of a church. A church constitution projects a self-image that can be either liberating for ministry or the very shackles that keep the machinery for mission from moving.[3]

The purpose of the church is to grow. It is God's plan that his people grow up: "Grow in the grace and knowledge of our Lord and Savior Jesus Christ" (II Peter 3:18). "No longer . . . children, tossed to and fro and carried about with every wind of doctrine . . . we are to grow up in every way " (Eph. 4:14, 15). Hebrews 5:12-13, 14 says, "You need milk, not solid food; for everyone who lives on milk is unskilled in the word of righteousness . . . but solid food is for the mature." (See also I Cor. 3:2; I Peter 2:2.) The purpose of the church is to enable God's people to grow into mature Christians.

It is also the purpose of the church to grow out. That the New Testament church understood this is abundantly clear from the book of Acts. The Christians of the first century sought every opportunity to allow God to use them in the expansion of his kingdom. Jesus said, "Go therefore and make disciples of all nations" (Matt. 28:19). The church is to be gathered and then scattered, as people come forth from worship and go everywhere, preaching the Good News.

The constitution of a congregation may be either mission-oriented or maintenance-oriented. The structure of a board may or may not be along the lines of New Testament principles. The New Testament does not give a great deal of direction for principles of organization, but several principles do apply. Is the church organized around the Great Commission? Are people serving in ways that reflect their spiritual gifts? Are boards, committees, leaders, and staff people held accountable? Does the church structure reflect opportunities for goal setting and review? Is good stewardship an important aspect in practice, as well as in theory?

The constitution reflects the philosophy of ministry of a congregation to a greater degree than most people would be willing to admit. It not only mirrors a congregation's self-image, but helps to form it. The constitution is a very important document which either contributes to church health or fouls up effective implementation of the Great Commission.

What Do the Signs Say?

The Church Building

Have you ever visited a large church and discovered, after parking your car, that you couldn't figure out which door to use? Churches are notorious for failing to put up signs. You can't find the sanctuary. You can't find the main office. You try a dozen doors, and most are locked. The experience may not tell you what is included in that church's philosophy of ministry, but it gives you a clue as to what is not included: sensitivity to visitors.

Many aspects of a church building can give hints about the congregation's philosophy of ministry. The very fact that the pastor's office is called a study gives at least an impression of the church's traditional priorities. If the pastor is supplied with a four-by-four foot closet for an office, it may be evidence of the philosophy of those who planned the building. Perhaps they thought very little of the pastor; or perhaps they expected the pastor to be out doing ministry rather than sitting behind a desk.

The grounds around a building tend to give clues about a congregation's self-image. If the church campus is full of weeds, untrimmed bushes, and long grass, the church may have a low self-image. Perhaps the shabbiness reflects a dying church. Maybe the church cares very little for neighborhood beauty. Whatever the grounds tell the visitor—and the church member—they do say something.

Even adjacent buildings can communicate enormously significant messages. The Church of the Shepherd was an urban church led by a young energetic pastor. Though the community had changed racially, the pastor, staff, and lay leaders had worked very hard to promote a healthy self-image in the congregation. There was much emphasis on mission and outreach. The congregation, though reluctant at first, had begun to see God's plan for them in a neighborhood full of new but different people. Fears of urban blight were laid aside.

Then it happened. The family in the big house directly across from the church moved. A buyer was not found immediately, so the house was boarded up. The communication of this "visual aid" was devastating. The self-image of the church people plunged. Even though the boards on the windows were temporary, a loud and clear message was given those who saw that house when they came to worship: "The neighborhood is going downhill!" Whether or not the conclusion was accurate was beside the point. It affected the congregation's self-image, promoting a negative philosophy of ministry.

Church architecture can communicate a church's philosophy of ministry and should be carefully considered any time a congregation plans to build. Does the building suggest openness, mission, outreach? Or is it a foreboding castlelike fortress? Is it bright and cheerful inside, representing joy and newness of life? Or is it an old dark musty dungeon?

It is interesting, but tragic, that so many church buildings are patterned after European cathedrals of the Middle Ages. For people with a European heritage, that kind of architecture may connote tradition and stability. But to others, such a style may communicate an imported, out-of-date religion. What kind of philosophy of ministry—what kind of self-image—does the church building communicate?

Buildings can give important first impressions. Second Methodist Church had a large spacious office, typical of a big-city church. The high ceiling was a brilliant white, with fancy sculptured plaster around the edges. The lights looked like upside-down umbrellas, hanging about three feet from the ceiling. There were several secretarial desks in the background, but between the lobby and the secretaries was a large counter about four feet high, with little windows on top and frosted glass between the windows. In the back of the room was a gigantic floor-to-ceiling vault. The place looked like a bank! What a first impression for the visitor! All it needed was a few cash registers, and they could have sold indulgences!

The Church's Name

Even the name of a congregation gives people some idea of its self-image. The Missionary Church of Jesus Christ may tell people about the priorities of the congregation. Fellowship Baptist Church may indicate the importance of love, friendship, and friendliness. The name can reflect a central doctrine—Trinity Lutheran Church; or a form of ministry and source of doctrine—Saint Paul's Episcopal.

Even spelling can reveal something. When the medium is the message, it is important to look with scrutiny at certain names. Our Saviour Church, spelled in the old English of the King James Bible, may communicate the name, but to some it may signal also that the congregation or the religion is behind the times.

The Church's Letterhead

This is another form of communication. If sloppy or poorly printed, it may communicate the congregation's self-image. Furthermore, the style of letters and boldness of type also could say something about how the congregation views itself. It may make a difference if the letterhead has a picture of the church, a picture of Christ, or a map of the church's location.

Whether or not a congregation's philosophy of ministry is accurately represented by the letterhead is not the issue. The point is that the mail going out of the church office communicates something, even before the actual letter is typed.

The Pastor's Office

Although alluded to above as part of the building, the pastor's office and its appearance will communicate a message about the ministry he or she performs. If it seems warm and comfortable, with nice furniture arranged for unobstructed communication, there is a good possibility that the pastor conducts a meaningful counseling ministry. If the walls are lined with bookshelves, the office projects the image of an educated person—perhaps a teaching ministry is a top priority.

If the desk is a mess of papers with stacks of books and mail, the ministry may be in a mess. Perhaps the congregation is not well organized; or perhaps the pastor does not have administrative gifts but there is someone else who administers the programs.

I once had some legal work to be done. Someone recommended a particular attorney, so I made an appointment. When I walked into his office, I was amazed to see papers and files piled so high he could barely see over the mountainous mess. I was so afraid he would misplace my legal documents that I had a copy made before I gave him the originals. Sure enough, several weeks later we were supposed to have another meeting, but we couldn't—he had lost the papers!

The Church's Location

The geographic location of a congregation is important. It gives a message. If the church is downtown in a large metropolitan area, it may be a central meeting place for the affairs of a particular church body. It also may be committed to the city. The ministry could reflect high priorities of time devoted to civic affairs.

A congregation located outside the downtown area could reflect the self-image of the neighborhood. If the building is visible to traffic patterns, it is in a good location. Church growth teaches the importance of high visibility and adequate parking.

One church in upstate New York combined a good location with excellent architecture. The back of the church faces a major artery of a busy, growing city. Most of the back wall is glass, so that those who pass by can see through to the front of the church, where a large cross is lighted. The message that congregation presents is inviting and welcoming for all who pass by. No visitor would be apprehensive about entering that building. Everyone in town has seen the inside, whether they actually have been there or not.

The Sanctuary

The relatively few moments a Christian spends in formal worship every Sunday are often the most important moments of the week. That is where the worshiper is fed and commissioned to do ministry in his or her world. What does the sanctuary communicate about the self-image of the church? As one looks around, what does it say about the beliefs and attitudes of the group that worships there? Is it clean? Is it modern? Is it traditional? Does it give a feeling of welcome?

One church was built with glass dividers at the rear of the sanctuary. Originally, the chairs behind the glass were for parents with toddlers and babies. But as the church grew, it became an overflow area, so now the last people to arrive must sit behind the glass and listen to worship over the speakers.

Who is usually last to arrive at a worship service? Visitors! People unfamiliar with the church have trouble finding it—that makes them late. They do not plan enough time to get there, because this is their first visit. They do not have an established time schedule for Sunday morning. Since they are late, they usually have to walk quite a distance because the parking lot is full. The church is also full, and they end up sitting behind the glass. What a wecome!

The sanctuary says a lot about our attitudes. It reflects the worship-image of the people of God. Are there flowers? Is the carpet worn? Are there banners? Is the sanctuary in need of paint? All such signs reflect the philosophy of ministry of the congregation.

The Worship Service

The form of worship in many congregations is established by people steeped in the tradition of the church. While that may be very important, every congregation also must be sensitive to the new Christian and to the visitor. If the worship service communicates in old English, does that perhaps communicate more than the church wants to say? Does God speak in "thees" and "thous"?

The New Testament was written in common Greek for the common man. The great Reformers translated hymns into the contemporary vernacular of their day. They set the hymns to the modern music of their time. Unfortunately, many churches of *this* century are still stuck in *that* century. What message does the medium give? Does it say God is antiquated? Does the form simply reflect the "good old tradition" so comfortable to repeat every year? The church needs to take a sharp look at Jesus' remarks to the Pharisees and scribes. Jesus condemned the church people of his day because they were playing church, caught in a religious rut. They were mired so deeply in traditional muck that they missed the Messiah altogether.

What does the worship service say about the congregation's self-image? Is the church interested in form, or in meaning? When religion becomes meaningless, it is time for another Reformation. Does the worship communicate a living Lord relevant for today? What does the service say about the people's attitudes toward their faith? What does it communicate about their philosophy of ministry?

"Signs, signs, everywhere signs!" Wherever there are churches, there are signs that tell about their ministry. The signs aren't formal. Many aren't intended. Some tell it like it is; others give the wrong impression. But all tell a story. They tell about the personality of a Body of Christ. They reflect the ecclesiastical image of the congregation. They say something about its philosophy of ministry.

There is no question about whether a local church has a philosophy of ministry. Every church has one. But how can a philosophy of ministry be used for growth?

There are many ways to use a philosophy of ministry, but to put it to work, a church must first recognize its self-image. Members with church-growth eyes might want to change their church's philosophy of ministry so that the congregation can be used more effectively to fulfill the Great Commission. But before a philosophy of ministry can be changed, it must be discovered. And in order to discover it, the people must find its origin.

Discussion Questions for Chapter II

1. What nonverbal messages does your church send to the community around it?

 ____

 ____

 ____

 ____

 ____

2. Analyze the time spent by discussion-group members in serving the congregation. Add up all the hours for the last week or month. What percentage was maintenance-related work? What percentage was mission- and outreach-related?
   Maintenance-oriented work: ____________%
   Mission- and outreach-oriented work: ____________%
   What does this say about your actual philosophy of ministry, as compared to the Lord's Great Commission?

   ____

   ____

   ____

   ____

   ____

3. What concrete goals and long-range plans are a regular part of the board and committee meetings at your church? List the boards and committees and their specific activities that reflect an emphasis on church growth.

Board or Committee	Activities That Reflect Church Growth
______________	____________________________
______________	____________________________
______________	____________________________
______________	____________________________
______________	____________________________
______________	____________________________

4. What percentage of the church budget is geared to outreach? What percentage is designated for maintenance? What areas are difficult to analyze? Does this say something about the categories you could use when constructing your budget in the future?
   Outreach-oriented money: ____________%
   Maintenance-oriented money: ________________%
5. What does your church constitution say about your ecclesiastical personality?

   ____

   ____

   ____

   ____

6. Pretend you are a visitor, taking a tour of your church building and grounds. List ways a visitor's first impression could be improved.

   ____

   ____

   ____

   ____

   ____

III

The Origin of Identity

Scientific study of the human body has unveiled some beautiful mysteries of the most complex organism made by God. What makes you uniquely you? Science teaches that most of a person's identity comes through chromosomes or genes in traits that are passed from generation to generation. The whole process is extremely complex—part of the creative miracle God performs in each and every human being.

Sociologists teach that much of our individuality comes also from learned behavior: Environment helps to shape attitudes and beliefs. The Scripture recognizes the importance of this learned behavior: "Train up a child in the way he should go, and when he is old he will not depart from it" (Prov. 22:6). A philosophy of life often reflects what a person was taught as a child.

It seems that a combination of factors from both within and without make each person unique. These factors shape and mold people into what they become as adults. Futhermore, people continue to change as various influences touch their lives. All these things form people's beliefs and attitudes. They also form the basis for a philosophy of ministry.

The Body of Christ, also, is very complex. Church growth experts emphasize this again and again. Analyzing the Body of Christ is a serious task which requires specialists in diagnostic techniques. The realization of the complexity of the Body of Christ is one reason many churches are making use of trained consultants who study a congregation to find symptoms of health or disease. They look at a church with X-ray perspective and see what the untrained eye cannot see. The trained diagnostician looks at the Body of Christ much as a physician looks at a human body.

A good friend of mine is a specialist in radiology, trained in diagnosing problems on the basis of X-rays. His office is in one of the hospitals I frequently visited to see patients and minister to them. Each time I came I would stop to say hello. One day he was busy examining an X-ray, and I asked him which part of the body we were looking at. I couldn't tell. Before he had a chance to explain, in walked a young intern. I was introduced as Dr. Hunter, and we shook hands. Just then my friend was called out of the office, but before he left, he asked the young intern to look at the X-ray and diagnose the problem.

After a few minutes of intense study, the intern turned to me and said, "I'm not sure, but I think the problem is right here." He pointed to the upper right-hand corner. Then he said, "What do you think, Dr. Hunter?"

Suddenly I realized he was confused by my title, but I thought it would be a great opportunity to have some fun. So I pointed to the middle left of the X-ray and said, "No, I think the problem is here."

When my friend came back, he asked the intern if he had found the problem. The intern pointed to the upper right and was told he was wrong. Then he pointed to the spot I had picked, and it turned out to be correct!

Purely by chance, I had guessed the problem area. Certainly no one would want to perform surgery on my advice! My training does not include diagnosis of problems in the human body.

When a church growth diagnostician looks at a Body of Christ, it can be seen that many factors contribute to the basic attitudes and beliefs of any local congregation. Like the human body, some influences originate within, while others come from outside. Determining the philosophy of ministry of a congregation, dissecting its identity, is a complex task. It begins back in the genealogies of the members.

Role Models

A role model is an example on which a person patterns his or her behavior. Parents, teachers, Sunday school teachers, pastors, and Scout leaders are primary role models. These people demonstrate behaviors and beliefs that a person might like to copy.

For example, a young boy may think of his father as a great athlete. Sports are stressed in home and school, with achievement viewed as top priority. Perhaps Dad was a football or basketball star in high school or college. As the child grows older, he may strive to emulate that sports-hero model.

There are various role models that help to shape the attitudes and the philosophy of ministry of a congregation.

Previous Churches

People who join a church by transfer bring with them all sorts of expectations. If a former church had a very low priority for Bible study, members of that congregation may bring that low priority with them. Unless it is challenged, it could be an infectious philosophy for their new church. This is especially true if many people with that attitude should join the congregation.

From a positive perspective, transferred people also can carry a healthy infection. For example, if several people transfer from churches where active evangelism is a high priority, they can bring that philosophy with them. If such people become a dominant force in the membership, they can affect the philosophy of ministry of their new church. This is positive, however, only if active evangelism is part of the desired philosophy of ministry of the new congregation. If it is not, tension and active resistance may result, much like the internal war of antibodies in the human body when an infectious element is introduced.

Scripture is like vitamins for the Body of Christ. When members are feeding on God's Word and living as the Body of Christ according to their gifts, the Body's resistance is built up against a sick philosophy of ministry. The people are less prone to be "carried about . . . by the cunning of men, by their craftiness in deceitful wiles" (Eph. 4:14).

Indoctrination can be considered a negative term because such an activity is frequently used in a manipulative way. As a positive term, the word means *teaching in* or *instructing in*. Healthy churches often have a series of instruction classes, even for those who transfer from other churches of the same denomination. One of the most important resources for such classes is a written philosophy of ministry.

Tradition

Tradition is another factor that serves as a role model for a philosophy of ministry. Every church has a tradition.

When a brand new congregation comes into existence and has its first worship service, traditions already are being formed—sometimes in inflexible steel. The new congregation worships at 9:00 A.M. on Sunday morning. It has formed a tradition. The pastor wears a gown. This has begun a tradition. Pews are bolted to the floor. A tradition has been cast.

Tradition sets the attitudes and beliefs of a congregation more than is realized. How many times has it been said, "But we've always done it that way!" Pastors perpetuate policies; boards and committees repeat programs. The cycle moves on and on.

Tradition can be good or bad. In the good sense, it can provide stability. In an unstable world, people look to the church for something solid and dependable. Tradition is history, with many lessons provided so that Christians can learn from the past. It is not good sense to repeat mistakes. A philosophy of ministry based on good solid tradition has a wealth of experience and a proven track record behind it.

When does tradition become a negative factor? Tradition turns sour when it loses its meaning, when the holy habit becomes an empty rut. The members of Zion Church had always been in the habit of standing and singing hymn No. 441 after the offering. That was a good habit because the words of the hymn were very appropriate for the giving of tithes and offerings. The congregation had been standing and singing 441 for fifty years. It had become a meaningless rut for many people. Once, on a stewardship Sunday, the pastor decided to place the hymn at a different point in the service for added emphasis. At the opening notes of hymn 441 on the organ, the whole congregation stood up! Like Pavlov's dogs, the congregation was trained for conditioned response. The meaning had been lost.

When neighborhoods change, so should philosophies of ministry. But often tradition itself prevents a relevant witness. An established, traditionally German congregation found itself in a community quickly turning Hispanic. The women's groups in the church decided to have a supper and invite the community, as a gesture of mission and outreach. They were disappointed when only a handful of Hispanic people responded. They were quite discouraged until someone pointed out that their well-advertised meal of knackwurst and sauerkraut was not what the people of the community desired. Tradition had blinded them to the realities of change.

Jesus faced a traditional church during his ministry on earth. The Pharisees and Sadducees had heaped rule upon regulation to the point that rules had lost all meaning in their lives. Religion had become irrelevant. The very fact of the Incarnation—Jesus in the flesh—is God's demanding statement that he wants to be relevant. Those Jews who followed Jesus the Messiah underwent an enormous change in philosophy of ministry.

Tradition is a strong determining factor in a congregation's philosophy of ministry. Self-images are heavily determined by the past. Present priorities and practices frequently have deep roots in history. A healthy congregation tests its philosophy of ministry to determine whether it continues to be God's will for the present time and in the particular location. It must be relevant. It must be effective in terms of making disciples and building the Body to maturity in Christ.

Denomination

The denomination of which a church is a member has a great influence on its philosophy of ministry. Congregational management, leadership expectations, policies, and priorities often are formed at denominational levels. Some denominations place a strong emphasis on evangelism. Others have specified social service as a main theme. Still others focus on activity in the ecumenical movement. While each local church is usually autonomous, there is power behind the denominational ability to influence a congregation's philosophy of ministry. That influence is seen in the three major ways.

Many denominations train pastors in denominational seminaries. The influence of the pastor will be discussed later. At this point, it is important to recognize the role the denomination plays in shaping priorities and programs through the pastor. Pastors do not stop learning when they leave the seminary. Yet for a majority of pastors, formidable ideas for ministry have been firmly fixed before they reach the congregational setting.

The denomination also designates long-range plans and goals. As they assemble in conventions, denominational bodies determine policies that usually filter down through the hierarchy to the local congregations. These priorities are then promoted through denominational programs, in films, and in periodicals and other literature.

Denominations often promote their programs and priorities through their publishing companies. Sunday school materials, vacation Bible school packets, adult learner's guides, hymnbooks, orders of service, pastoral handbooks, and Bible study aids are only a few of the many items that explicitly or implicitly help shape the beliefs and attitudes that form the image and identity of a congregation.

Many of those involved in the Church Growth Movement recognize the importance of the denomination. If a church growth philosophy of ministry is to have any local vitality, it must also be supported by the denomination.

Many denominational leaders are being trained in church growth principles. Most major denominations have produced an introductory book on the subject of church growth, written from the perspective of the denomination. Seminaries are beginning to offer courses in church growth for pastors and lay people. Some denominations are setting up an office of church growth as a coordinating agency, and their publishing companies are printing materials permeated with church growth principles.

Theological Emphases

Theological emphases can serve as role models for a philosophy of ministry. Some churches have a particular theological stance—predestination, for example. Such a doctrine will have an effect upon the church's philosophy of ministry and will help to determine priorities relating to evangelism or social ministry. The importance of baptism or the Lord's Supper is stressed in some denominations more than others. A congregation with a priority for a sacramental ministry will conduct a ministry strongly along those lines. Churches that emphasize experiences or "feelings" will have programs of instruction and worship services that are geared accordingly.

Community Church has a strong theological view of ministry which places responsibility on each person. In this church, members have developed their spiritual gifts and are taking an active part—not only in church work but in acts of ministry. Their very identity has been shaped by a theological conviction.

On the other hand, Valley Church stresses the importance of the pastoral office. Here the lay people are assigned tasks at the pastor's discretion. The pastor is seen as a shepherd-director and is viewed as "the only one who can actually do ministry in the real sense. Otherwise, what would happen to good church order?" This theological position in regard to the pastorate affects the church's philosophy of ministry.

Church growth recognizes the importance of a theological base. A church growth person possesses a theological conviction: It is God's will that the church grow. Church growth implicitly articulates an incarnational theology that moves a person to mission, a comprehensive task that includes redemption and sanctification. A strong ecclesiology characterizes the Church Growth Movement: The church is seen not as an institution but as the living presence of Jesus Christ in the world. The centrality of Christ as both Savior and Lord is the focal point of church growth. Emphasis on the gifts of the Spirit stimulates involvement of the laity, and accountability as it relates to the doctrine of stewardship is part of the life of both the individual and the church. The importance of the Word of God is a constant emphasis. God's grace and forgiveness through the cross are the life-blood stimulus for the growing church.

These various models—previous churches, tradition, denomination, and theological emphases—influence the attitudes and image of the local church; they shape and direct programs and priorities. However, these models are not the only factors that serve as origins of identity for a church.

Gift Mixes and Leadership Styles

The church is not an institution, not just a building made of stone and wood. The church building at Fifth and Main could burn down this week. The people could have the rubble bulldozed aside and gather for worship in the cleared space. The church lives on. The church is people.

Scripture uses many symbols to describe the church. When

the Bible speaks of the church as a building, it is referring to a living building. The people who make up the church are living stones, with Jesus Christ as the chief cornerstone (Eph. 2:20). The symbol of the body also is a popular New Testament image for the church. Jesus Christ is the head, and the people are the members of his body (Col. 1:18; Rom. 12:4).

There is no question about it: Jesus Christ is of central importance to the church. He is the King of his kingdom, the Chief Priest of the worshiping community, the Shepherd of his sheep, the Bridegroom to the bride. When it comes to the identity of a church, however, we cannot deny that the people are also very important. And since the people of a church are important, their gift mix and leadership styles shape the church's philosophy of ministry.

A gift mix is that particular set of spiritual gifts given to the people whom God draws together in a congregation. Every Christian has at least one spiritual gift. Collectively, a church has the gifts the Lord needs to meet the challenges before that congregation. Some members discover, develop, and use their spiritual gifts. Others are more immature in their spiritual life: They have not grown to the point where they have activated the gifts given to them. Still others are determined to remain babes in the faith. They are nominal Christians who are not growing, and unless evangelized and rekindled, they will not discover their gifts. Consequently, the collective gift mix of any congregation will be based only on those members who use their spiritual gifts. This is what helps to shape a congregation's identity.

Leadership style is another important factor of influence in the church. Leadership styles can be evaluated by either a *development* or an *orientation* method.

Development

In industry there is a hierarchy of leadership roles, beginning at the bottom with the unskilled worker and ending at the top with the chairperson of the board (see Figure 4). Each leadership role is different. In industrial terms, positions 6 to 9 focus on production, while positions 1 to 6 focus on management. The foreman has a foot in each world. To put these industrial terms into the terminology of the church, perhaps the work roles are more helpful than the position titles. A church doesn't have a chairperson of the board in the industrial management sense, but a church should have one person or a group of people who work to develop leaders.

Development Method

	Position	Roles of Work
Focus on Management	1. Board Chairperson	develops leaders
	2. Board Level	overall production
	3. Topline Management	long-term planning and profit concerns
	4. Middle Management	evaluation and long-term planning
	5. Supervisor	works on goals
Focus on Management / Focus on Production	6. Foreman	begins to do some planning
Focus on Production	7. Lead Worker	skilled worker, set-up person, lays out work
	8. Skilled Worker	functioning skill, knows the job
	9. Unskilled Worker	

Figure 4

The development of leadership styles is at various levels in different congregations. In some churches, all the people are unskilled workers. They do not know their gifts, have not taken ownership of a ministry within the congregation, and perhaps never think about anything but perpetuating the programs of the past. There is no overall sense of mission or direction. On the other hand, a congregation could have many people involved in evaluation, effectiveness, goal setting, and advance planning.

The degree to which the people are involved in the development of leadership styles will reflect to some extent the church's philosophy of ministry. A church with little development usually will have a ministry that leans toward maintenance. The church with a developed leadership will lean toward a ministry of mission.

Orientation

A philosophy of ministry is determined also by the orientation of the people. In management terminology, people tend to be either goal-oriented or relationship-oriented. This is sometimes represented by an orientation grid, with a vertical axis representing relationships and a horizontal axis representing goals (see Figure 5). A goal-oriented person (A)

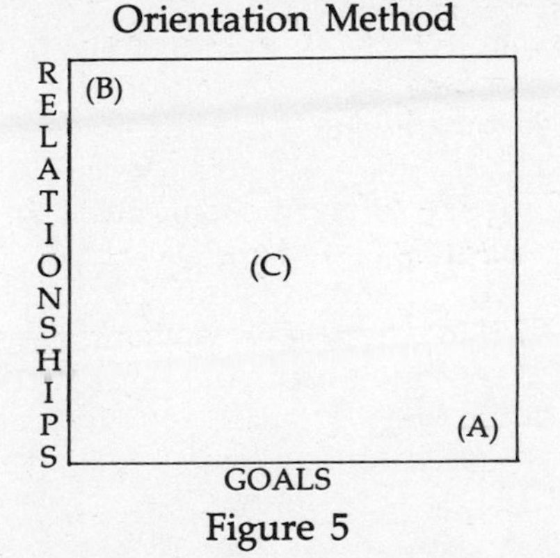

Figure 5

would fall toward the goal axis, while one who is more relationship-oriented (B) would fall toward the relationship axis. A person with equal concern for goals and relationships (C) would be a compromise-type person.

Since people are attracted to others who are like themselves, congregations frequently are made up of many who are goal-oriented or, at the other extreme, relationship-oriented. No person is one extreme or the other all the time, but there often is a tendency to lean one way or the other in overall decision-making behavior.

Congregations with a majority of relationship-oriented people tend to have a philosophy of ministry that leans toward fellowship. It is a relational, warm, family-type congregation. Congregations with a majority of goal-oriented people have a more program-oriented philosophy of ministry.

Doesn't every congregation really include a lot of different types of people, in terms of gift mix and leadership styles? Yes. Therefore we must concentrate on those who tend to set the tone of philosophy of ministry for the rest: *the pastor* and *the leaders*.

The Pastor

The Pastor is a strong influence in the philosophy of ministry of a congregation. Church growth teaches that the pastor is the person with the most influence on the direction of the church. In *Your Church Can Grow,* C. Peter Wagner says that "in America, the primary catalytic factor for growth in a local church is the pastor."[1]

The church growth pastor must understand his or her own gift mix, thank God for it, and perform a ministry accordingly. Such pastors will recognize areas in which they are not gifted and see that other staff people are added or lay people mobilized, so that ministry is adequately accomplished in all areas and needs of congregational life.

The gift mix of the head pastor will help shape the philosophy of ministry for the congregation. If, for example, a minister has spiritual gifts in pastoring and exhortation, a strong counseling ministry may dominate the church programs. If a pastor has the gift of faith—that supernatural ability to face the unconquerable boldly—the church may take on great challenges in the name of Jesus Christ and the glory of his kingdom.

The pastor's leadership style also will influence the identity of the church. Church growth acknowledges, for example, that those ministers with a relationship orientation tend to pastor congregations that remain around two hundred members. This is because the philosophy of ministry tends toward being "one big happy family," and the people realize that if the "family" gets any bigger, they will lose that intimacy.

Most church growth pastors have a leadership style at least at the level of foreman. They begin to be involved in planning as well as short-term and long-term goal setting. They focus on management of the people's gifts, and they see as their goal the development of good stewardship for the effective implementation of the Great Commission. Pastors who are involved in church growth move beyond *programmatic* skill levels—What program can I use on my people? They develop a skill level that becomes *innovative*. They begin to bend programs to fit their own situation. They are interested in evaluation: Was what we accomplished effective? Church growth pastors move up to a level of *congregational leadership*. They begin to plan in terms of concepts. They see visions and dream dreams. They develop leaders. At this level, pastors intentionally begin to seek to determine a philosophy of ministry.

The Leaders

The leaders of the congregation greatly affect the philosophy of ministry. This is especially true of the "founding fathers." Lyle Schaller speaks of them as the pioneers.[2] They were there first. They started the tradition, even in terms of philosophy of ministry.

The leaders have a certain gift mix that influences the attitudes of the congregation. Those who have the gift of service may dominate the leadership. Calvary Church had a strong leadership core of people with gifts of service and help. Whenever there was a community need, these leaders teamed together to meet that need. The church gained a reputation for action, Christian love toward the community, and service to those in need. The congregation established a philosophy of ministry based on the gift mix of its leadership. One only needs to think of the philosophy of ministry of the Salvation Army to realize the tremendous influence of its founding leader, William Booth.

The orientation and style of leadership contribute to a congregation's philosophy of ministry in a major way. A growth-oriented congregation will see the need for discovering levels of leadership styles among those who work on its boards and committees. It will emphasize the importance of developing and training leaders for the health and growth of God's kingdom, as he uses them to make disciples.

Location/Environment

Just as the environment into which someone is born affects that person's identity, the locality of a congregation affects its philosophy of ministry.

East Saint Louis, Illinois, is across the Mississippi River from the bright, renewed downtown streets of its sister city in Missouri. The Saint Louis Arch gleams in the sunshine on the west side of the river. Only a few miles away, but miles apart in life-style, is the high crime, dirty, industrial section of East Saint Louis. Unity Church has a small but significant ministry in its neighborhood. It probably never will be the largest congregation in the denomination or draw national attention. But day after day, the church serves the cause of Christ according to its own philosophy of ministry.

The congregation found itself in a community with teenage crime running rampant. When it saw an opportunity to build a youth program, a gymnasium was utilized. Seminary students worked with the neighborhood youth. While playing basketball, Christian witness was verbally given. Young people were invited to church. Some took instruction classes and joined the church. Jesus Christ, through the channel of basketball, transformed some lives.

Not far away, on the west side of Saint Louis, is the elite suburb of Ladue. The Christian Church in that locality could not reach their youth with basketball. Those young people had cars, horses, ski weekends, parties—a full calendar. A different ministry was needed. The youth there needed genuine adult friendship, since many of the jet-set parents found little time to be with their children. They needed a friend who would give them personal attention. A strong counseling ministry provided avenues for Christ to heal and direct lives in a relevant way. On a clear day, a resident of Ladue can look east and see the Saint Louis Arch. The two congregations are not that far apart—or are they?

Church philosophies change with locality because people change with locality. This further determining influence on a philosophy of ministry has to do with the *felt needs* of the people who are the church's target of ministry.

Robert Schuller is well known for his advice for growing churches: "Find a hurt and heal it."[3] Some people see that comment as secular marketing advice. Actually, it is part of God's design to be incarnate in people's lives. Jesus Christ always sought to be relevant. He knew what the woman at the well wanted—water! (John 4:7-30). He wasn't content that she receive only ordinary water; he was compelled to tell her about living water. Yet he began by meeting her felt need.

Church growth teaches that a philosophy of ministry should be sensitive to the needs of the people to whom the church is ministering. From place to place, that will be drastically different. The gospel doesn't change. The Lord is the same yesterday, today, and forever (Heb. 13:8). But the stage for relevant witness will change from scene to scene.

Transitory Philosophy

Since the world is in a constant state of upheaval, it is essential that a congregation review its philosophy of ministry regularly. Once a year church leaders should take inventory, evaluating their current philosophy. An objective look should be taken at all factors that influence church identity. Neighborhoods change, church leaders change, pastors change.

Is the philosophy of ministry up-to-date? Is it on target for the church at this time? Does it reflect optimum effectiveness of the congregation's mission? These are the tests with which a philosophy of ministry should be regularly scrutinized.

Discussion Questions for Chapter III

1. What are some role models that have influenced your understanding of the church's purpose and priorities?

____

____

____

____

____

____

2. What identity for the church was reflected by each model listed above? Are they positive, or negative, in terms of church growth? Are they biblical?

____

____

____

____

____

____

3. Some members of your group previously may have belonged to other congregations. Ask them to contrast their previous church's identity and image with the one to which they now belong. List these differences to see the uniqueness of your congregation.

___

___

___

___

4. What would you list as the unique characteristics of your denomination? Are these characteristics conducive to the stimulation of church growth?

___

___

___

5. What are the theological emphases at your church? Review the materials for Sunday school and member instruction. What are the priorities? Do they include evangelism, church growth, outreach, spiritual gifts, stewardship accountability, and worldwide mission efforts? How do they define the image of the church—as a bureaucracy, as an institution, or as a living organism?

___

___

___

6. Does your church motivate and equip leaders according to a good understanding of gift mixes and leadership styles? If not, what concrete steps could be taken to implement a good strategy for finding God's leaders among his people?

7. Describe your church's location. List ways you think the location has helped develop your philosophy of ministry.

IV

A Theology for Establishing a Philosophy of Ministry

Why should a church have an expressed philosophy of ministry? It is practical. It is helpful. It communicates. But is it biblical? Yes! There are four major theological reasons for a church to express its philosophy of ministry.

To Declare How Its Ministry Fits into God's Plan

Jesus said that he is the Vine and his people are the branches (John 15:1-11). A philosophy of ministry should be a confession of connection: Christians are attached to Jesus Christ, the Vine. They *do* receive strength from him. Without him, the Christian does not have life.

Since God's people are attached to the Vine, they acknowledge that it is a natural part of their life-style to bear fruit. The fruit itself is a witness to the Vine. His strength and power make a significant difference in people's lives. A philosophy of ministry is a declaration that believers are an extension of Christ in this world.

A philosophy of ministry also should be a confession of connection: Christians are attached to Jesus Christ, the Vine. They *do* receive strength from him. Without him, the Christian does not have life.

A philosophy of ministry also should explain at what point

the people are attached to the Vine. It is a confession that while all the branches have a common Vine and bear similar fruit, no two branches are the same. Yet every branch is part of God's ongoing plan of salvation, and a philosophy of ministry will recognize this.

George Peters points to the history of God's redemptive plan.[1] In the Old Testament, God's concern for the nations was administered through his chosen people, Israel. The mission of Israel was *centripetal.* As a "sacred magnetism," Israel lived in the presence of the Lord and drew the attention of the nations toward their God. Their particular philosophy of ministry was nationalistic in nature.

The promise was laid down in the covenant: God chose Israel as his people and promised to be their God (Exod. 19:5, 29:45). They looked forward to fulfillment of the promise—a messiah for the salvation of God's people.

In the New Testament, God's promise is fulfilled in Jesus Christ, and the mission becomes *centrifugal.* Whereas the philosophy of ministry was a "come" philosophy in the Old Testament, in the New Testament it becomes a "go" philosophy. The messengers are sent beyond the national dimensions to gather the New Israel.

Jesus Christ, sent by the Father, now sends his disciples to all nations to make disciples (Matt. 28:19-20). The change in mission from centripetal to centrifugal was a major change in philosophy of ministry.[2] It was not a change in ministry, however, but only a change in method. The history of salvation continues.

Any Christian philosophy of ministry will reflect the Triune God's relentless desire for a relationship with his people. From Genesis to Judgment, God desires his people to have life with him. His redemptive impetus is the continuing thread woven into the biblical record down through the ages—across cultures, changing form and location, on spiritual mountain-tops and in human fleshly valleys.

The redemptive mission is the constant; the philosophy of that mission, the variable. The ultimate goal remains the same—the redemption of people to our Creator. It is the form for reaching the people, the philosophy of ministry, that changes.

Moses was minding his own business when the Lord's philosophy of ministry called for a leader. Moses was called to reach God's people in Egypt so that their bondage to slavery would not continue. The philosophy of ministry was liberation, but it soon changed to exodus; then it became trust in God to provide nourishment in the desert. Finally, growing anticipation of the Promised Land became a reality as the people crossed the Jordon. The leaders changed. The identity of the ministry changed. But the redemptive concern of God for his people remained constant; that is one of the basic central themes for a philosophy of ministry. To acknowledge God's redemptive plan is to confess that his people are part of God's continual work of salvation.

To Proclaim Self-identity

A philosophy of ministry may express identity in a variety of ways. Churches can reflect their different localities, calls to particular kinds of work, different leaders, varieties of gift mixes, and different origins.

When describing who they are, churches may say they are Black or Hispanic, rural or suburban, blue-collar or intellectual. The "who" will vary. But self-identity always will be the same when we express "whose" we are. One of the constants of biblical theology is to profess to whom we belong. A philosophy of ministry is a vehicle for proclamation, a platform for expressing a relationship with God, who has called his people "out of darkness into his marvelous light" (I Peter 2:9). In this way, it illuminates the source of strength, the guidelines for living, the origin of forgiveness, and the Christian's hope for eternity. A philosophy of ministry will identify the people as *God's* people.

The covenant relationship was established by God, not by humans. God's people discover a God who comes looking for them. In spite of sin, God comes to us to forgive. In spite of separation, God comes to restore. In spite of bondage, God comes to free.

The covenant relationship finds concrete expression in Jesus Christ. God cares so much, he sent his Son (John 3:16). The grace of God is a constant foundation upon which a philosophy of ministry is built. It is a witness and testimony to the grace of God: "For by grace you have been saved through faith; and this is not of your own doing, it is the gift of God" (Eph. 2:8).

When a church declares to whom it belongs, it declares also the continuing presence of God through his Holy Spirit. The Holy Spirit calls God's people into relationship with him. He uses the Word as a means of declaring his presence. The gospel is the core of the church's testimony.

The Holy Spirit is the Spirit of power, the source of energy. A philosophy of ministry is only a paper doctrine unless the people are plugged into that power source. The Holy Spirit brings about essential changes in the very nature of people in the church. When they walk in the Spirit, they do not gratify the desires of the flesh (Gal. 5:16). The fruit they produce is fruit of the Spirit: love, joy, peace, patience, kindness, goodness, faithfulness, gentleness, self-control (Gal. 5:22-23).

Just as each person has a unique identity, each congregation is unique and can express its own identity through its philosophy of ministry. However, while each person is unique, there are some characteristics all people have in common: hearts, noses, eyes, feet. All churches have characteristics that are constant. The presence of the Spirit produces the fruit of the Spirit.

Whereas a philosophy of ministry is an expression of particularity in identity, it also is a declaration of unity: "There is one body and one Spirit, just as you were called to the one hope that belongs to your call, one Lord, one faith, one baptism, one God and Father of us all, who is above all and through all and in all" (Eph. 4:4).

Through baptism, people are born again into a spiritual eternal family. God is their Father. They share in the meal

Jesus Christ has provided. They are brothers and sisters in the faith. Their family name is Christian. They join Jesus in his prayer: "Holy Father! Keep them safe by the power of your name, the name you gave me, so that they may be one just as you and I are one" (John 17:11 TEV).

Regardless of the diversity of the philosophy of ministry of local churches, this central confession will demonstrate to whom Christians belong, for "he has delivered us . . . to the kingdom of his beloved Son, in whom we have redemption, the forgiveness of sins" (Col. 1:13-14).

To Demonstrate God's Revelation

A philosophy of ministry is a statement declaring the corporate belief that God is alive and active as he unveils himself in his activity in this world. It is a statement about the way God has revealed himself to a particular congregation; a concrete expression of the reality of the resurrected Christ and the power and presence of his Spirit.

When Beulah Church established a philosophy of ministry which included an experimental grade school, its declaration to the community was, "God has revealed this to be his will for us. Furthermore, he is going to use this ministry to reveal himself to children who attend this school, and to their families." The revelation of God takes shape and form through a philosophy of ministry that declares *how* God is using his people to reveal himself through mission and ministry.

The centrality of Christ in a philosophy of ministry is essential. Jesus Christ is the key to understanding the revelation of God. As the epitome of God's revelation of himself, he sent his Son into the world. In Jesus Christ, God broke into history in his incarnate presence. God, in Jesus, came into the world to fulfill his redemptive purpose—"to save sinners" (I Tim. 1:15). Christ, ministering in and through his Body, reveals the hope of life to the real world in a concrete way. God's love comes alive in Jesus Christ: "In this the love of God was made manifest among us, that God sent his only Son into the world, so that we might live through him" (I John 4:9).

The revelation of God is a spiritual experience in which God, through his Word and by the power of his Spirit, draws his people to himself and reveals himself to them. Revelation is something that happens *in* people, more than *to* people. The Apostle Paul writes in Romans 12:2, "Do not be conformed to this world but be transformed by the renewal of your mind, that you may prove what is the will of God, what is good and acceptable and perfect."

A declaration of God's revelation is a profession of his presence. It is not so much that people have come to know God, but that they have become known *by* him (Gal. 4:9). He calls them to himself, to a totally new birth and life, and through that, he reveals himself (John 3:3, 6). A philosophy of ministry that declares God's activity of revelation demonstrates that God is alive and active in and through his people—the church.

To Manage Effectively

A philosophy of ministry is a reflection of a theology of creation. Faith perceives that God has provided all the resources with which we are surrounded (Heb. 11:3). A theology of creation places ownership squarely in the hands of God: "In the beginning God created the heavens and the earth" (Gen. 1:1). Furthermore, God continues his creative activity down through the centuries as the Divine Provider for all people (Ps. 145:15-16).

It is God's world, but he has loaned it to his created people. The wise use of resources applies also to the ministry of the church. Some Christians have been very poor examples of effectiveness and efficiency in the church. In the area of building use alone, the world often has looked at the church with downright disgust. What corporation or business, large or small, would spend such enormous amounts of money on buildings that sit idle more than 90 percent of the time?

Once I visited a large congregation with an educational building a block long and two stories high. "Do you have a school?" I asked. The answer was no.

"Did you have a school at one time?" I asked. The answer was still no.

"What do you use this enormous building for?" I wondered out loud.

"It's used on Sunday mornings for our Sunday school and in the summer for vacation Bible school. Sometimes our youth uses part of the building."

I couldn't help thinking that they should start using the building more wisely, or God would surely take it away from these particular people and give it to someone else.

The doctrine of stewardship produces a responsible member of the kingdom of God, and this includes accountability. Church growth thinking does not accept the rather passive, unbiblical idea that God does not care about results. On the contrary, God goes to great lengths to reconcile us to himself (Rom. 8:32).

Jesus taught his disciples about results. He was concerned that the banquet table be filled (Luke 14:15-23). He wanted fig trees that produced figs (Luke 13:6-9). He wanted the plentiful harvest reaped (Matt. 9:36-38). In the parable of the good and faithful servant (Matt. 25:14-30), Jesus teaches that wise use of resources is imperative. A modern use of the term *stewardship* is *management*. The resources that God gives us really belong to him. His people are to manage them for the glory of his kingdom.

A philosophy of ministry helps a congregation become a good corporate steward of time, talents, and money. It will reflect intentionality of ministry: the directing of resources according to well-thought-out priorities. It will help a congregation focus on its identity: It will help the people discover who they are and who they are not. It will help show outsiders why that church is different from the one down the block. While each church has a different identity, attitude, and priorities, this foundation of concern for good stewardship will be a common theological basis for all churches that establish a philosophy of ministry.

Jesus' Philosophy of Ministry

Did Jesus have a philosophy of ministry? Careful observation would seem to indicate that he did. Though it was not written out, there was a distinct set of priorities and attitudes that provided precedence for his actions. This philosophy of ministry is recorded later in the Gospels. The centrality of the cross is clear: "For the Son of man also came not to be served but to serve" (Mark 10:45). Jesus was intentional about his mission. On the way to Jerusalem, he took his disciples aside and told them what was going to happen: "We are going up to Jerusalem; and the Son of man will be delivered to the chief priests and scribes, and they will condemn him to death, and deliver him to the Gentiles to be mocked and scourged and crucified, and he will be raised on the third day" (Matt. 20:18-19).

The Lord articulated a philosophy of ministry. He professed his identity and purpose not only to his disciples, but to those who gathered at the synagogue:

> The Spirit of the Lord is upon me,
> because he has anointed me to preach
> good news to the poor.
> He has sent me to proclaim release to the captives
> and recovering of sight to the blind,
> to set at liberty those who are oppressed,
> to proclaim the acceptable year of the Lord.
>
> Luke 4:18-19, quoting Isaiah 61:1-2

Jesus' ministry was church growth-oriented. He said plainly, "I will build my church" (Matt. 16:18). It is upon Jesus Christ, the Son of the living God, that the church was founded. His ministry was comprehensive, in that he was concerned with the whole person (Matt. 25:31ff.). Within that comprehensive framework, Jesus had priorities when it came to the forms of ministry. When he sent out the Twelve, for example, he charged them to "go nowhere among the Gentiles, and enter no town of the Samaritans, but go rather to the lost sheep of the house of Israel" (Matt. 10:5-6).

The sending of the Twelve and the sending of the seventy are examples of the way Jesus saw the forms of ministry to be performed. That sending also provides a theological base for a philosophy of ministry. Jesus informed the disciples about their calling when he said, "As the Father has sent me, even so I send you" (John 20:21). For that special calling they would receive the Holy Spirit (John 20:22). The extension of Jesus' ministry is real. He told his disciples, "If you forgive the sins of any, they are forgiven; if you retain the sins of any, they are retained" (John 20:23).

Perhaps these "sending" narratives provide an idea of Jesus' philosophy of ministry for those disciples and for that particular time (Matt. 10:1-20; Luke 9:1-6; Luke 10:1-23). There are several similarities in the narratives. In all three sections, the disciples are: (1) sent by the Lord; (2) to preach the kingdom (Luke 10 uses the Greek word for *say*); (3) to heal; (4) to move on and (apparently) not waste time if the people were not receptive; and (5) to travel light. In addition to these common factors, in Matthew 10 and Luke 9, Jesus expanded the healing ministry to include curing diseases and cleansing lepers. He also mentioned casting out demons. In Matthew 10 as well as Luke 10, Jesus reminded his followers that they would not have an easy task, since they were "like sheep among wolves."

When sending his disciples out, Jesus commanded them to do some specific tasks. In the Great Commission (Matt. 28:19-20), he told them to make disciples by baptizing in the name of the Father, the Son, and the Holy Spirit, and by teaching all that he had commanded them. Luke's Gospel includes the importance of repentance and forgiveness, to be proclaimed in the name of the risen Christ. Jesus' disciples were to be witnesses of his suffering, death, and resurrection to all nations (Luke 24:48; Acts 1:8; see also Mark 16:15).

It is apparent that there were some particular forms that expressed Jesus' philosophy of ministry. He had a specific mission and followed his priorities. He commanded his disciples to go to certain places at certain times to perform certain ministries. The early church demonstrated this philosophy of ministry throughout the book of Acts. As we observe the ministry of the apostles, we see that each had a philosophy of ministry; that all were common in theological foundation but differed in form and priorities (Gal. 2:7-9).

Indeed, the Christian church today is in a different setting. Yet the gospel is eternal. A philosophy of ministry for the local church is a contemporary statement of the eternal truths of God's Word, applied to the real world in a relevant way.

Discussion Questions for Chapter IV

1. Can you list ways your congregation officially or unofficially declares its place in God's redemptive activity?

___

___

___

___

2. On a scale from 1 to 10, how would your church's average members rate in awareness of personal involvement in God's redemptive activity? What steps could you take to raise their awareness level?

___

___

___

___

3. Does your church demonstrate a "come" (centripetal) style of ministry? What examples reflect this type of philosophy?

____

____

____

____

____

4. Does your congregation demonstrate a "go" (centrifugal) style of ministry? What examples reflect this type of philosophy?

____

____

____

____

____

5. When your church demonstrates its philosophy of ministry, does it reflect an aspect of a relationship with God? List examples.

____

____

____

____

6. In what areas of ministry is your congregation involved to reveal Christ to the unchurched? List the ministries and the ways Christ is revealed.

____

____

____

____

____

7. Do you agree that Jesus' ministry is church growth-oriented? If not, how do you disagree? If so, how would you expect the Lord to run your church today, using priorities for growth?

____

____

____

____

____

V

New Testament Images for a Biblical Philosophy of Ministry

While each congregation will differ, each philosophy of ministry will reflect an ecclesiology that is thoroughly biblical. An ecclesiology, the doctrine of the church, can be aimed at the Church universal or at a particular congregation. In the New Testament, most occurrences of the Greek word for *church*, *ecclesia*, refer to the local assembly of believers.

When they hear the word *church*, most people in our contemporary world seem to think of a building. When people talk about a church, they are often speaking of bricks and mortar, boards, nails, glass, steel, and whatever else it takes to construct a building. This is not what God has in mind when he talks about the church.

What is needed today is a massive effort to deprogram building-oriented Christians so they can see the living, beautiful organism that God has called into being, and of which they are a very special part. One of the great contributions of the Church Growth Movement is the reemphasis of a healthy image of the church. Church is not just a place where we go. It is that Body which God's people are, or can be, if they let God be God and have his way with their lives. The time is overdue for Christians to stop playing church. It is time to *be* the church.[1]

In baptism, a person is born again into a new relationship

with God, on the one hand and, on the other, with fellow brothers and sisters in the faith (Eph. 2:9). In baptism sins are washed away, and through the forgiveness of sins the believer becomes part of God's kingdom (Col. 1:13-14). The cross, with its power over sin and death, becomes a personal possession (Rom. 6:3). The Christian comes away from baptism with a garment of holiness which only Jesus possesses naturally: "For as many of you as were baptized into Christ have put on Christ" (Gal. 3:27).

God's call to people, his redemptive act personally applied to their lives, pulls them away from their old nature (Adam) and calls them to put on the new (Eph. 4:22-24). They no longer live for themselves, but for Christ, the Lord of the church and their personal King (II Cor. 5:14-15).

Baptism is part of the process of becoming one of Christ's disciples (Matt. 28:19-20). As a disciple, a member of the organism called a church, a person is in a living relationship with God. That relationship gives intimate newness of life to each person who, by repentance and faith, is reconciled through the cross (Eph. 2:14-16). It is a relationship that Scripture describes in a number of ways. A philosophy of ministry, if it is to be biblical, must be drawn from these biblical expressions of the nature of the church.

The Temple of God

At first it sounds as though the Bible is referring to a building on the corner of Fifth and Main. Bricks and mortar? Not this temple! This building is alive! The very power of God is the lifeblood of the church. The presence of God gives life to his people, who form a temple of living stones (I Peter 2:5). The church is not "the temple of God" in the sense that God lives there. God is everywhere (Jer. 23:24). It is God's temple because *he* calls it into existence. It belongs to *him*. And only *he* gives it life. If only all the boards, committees, councils, sessions, pastors, and members would keep that in mind!

God's people are built into this living structure. They are

joined together in the framework of this holy temple (Eph. 2:21-22). The cement is nothing less than the power of God. The people of God are workers together (I Cor. 3:9). Paul calls them a field, implying that there will be growth (I Cor. 3:8; Eph. 2:21). They are living stones because of Christ, *the* Living Stone who was precious in God's sight (I Peter 2:5).

A denomination is not the foundation for a church. A pastor and the leaders are not the foundation for a church. Jesus Christ, the Living Stone, is the foundation and the Chief Cornerstone (Eph. 2:20). *He* is the foundation for a church, and for any philosophy of ministry of any church.

But God's people are more than living stones. They are more than a corporate temple owned by God. As God's people, they are the place where God resides (I Cor. 3:16; Eph. 2:22). Many people in today's world have the idea that God lives in buildings of brick and mortar, or that he lives in heaven and doesn't care about the people in this world. Church growth, with its emphasis on the nature of the church, teaches that God is everywhere, and this includes his presence *in* people. The role of the church is nothing less than God's role in the world, through people who have been made into new wine skins to hold some new and very powerful wine—God's presence in the Holy Spirit (Matt. 9:17).

The Household of God

Closely related to the analogy of the temple of God is the idea that the church is the household of God. The nature of the church as God's household tells something about the church on the inside and, as it reaches out, reflects the Great Commission.

Looking at the household of God from the inside, Paul reminded the Ephesians that they were once without a home (Eph. 2:19). Since God's people are only passing through this world, they recognize that nothing is forever, that everything is temporary. As members of the church, they are part of an eternal household, fellow citizens with the saints of God down through the ages. They are in partnership with Abraham, Jeremiah, Barnabas and Paul, Jesus and the disciples.

Based on the Chief Cornerstone, Jesus Christ (Eph. 2:20), God's people have access to the Father. In unity, all believers are privileged to be able to reach the Creator of the universe (Eph. 2:18). This means they have power! Jesus said, "Whatever you ask the Father in my name, he may give it to you" (John 15:16).

In First Timothy 3:15, Paul gives some very good advice about how Christians should act. He says the church is the household of the living God, and those of the household should behave in a fitting manner. The church is "the pillar and bulwark of the truth." This truth, he goes on to explain, is the mystery that makes for godliness (v. 16).

Those who want to reflect upon a philosophy of ministry for their church would do well to note Paul's words in verse 16. This is the mystery that makes for godliness, as the members of God's household confess:

> He was manifested in the flesh,
> vindicated in the Spirit,
> seen by angels,
> preached among the nations,
> believed on in the world,
> taken up in glory.

What a tremendous confessional foundation for a church growth philosophy of ministry!

"He was manifested in the flesh."

Jesus is God in the flesh. It is God's desire to be incarnate, in the flesh, in this world. The household of faith, those who are in Christ, are not *of* the world, but *in* the world (John 17:14-15). God always has been intensely interested in touching people's lives. The church is called to a relevant ministry, meeting felt needs.

"He was vindicated in the Spirit."

Jesus Christ is justified before God. Through his cross and resurrection, believers, too, are justified before God. In contrast to the flesh, God's people can live by the Spirit. The church is not just another club or organization. It is a *spiritual* household, justified before God through the forgiveness of sins.

"He was seen by angels."

The great work of redemption was watched by the whole universe, a mighty experience of which Christians are a part. As the household of faith, God's people join Christ's ministry, watched by spiritual beings. First Peter 1:12, referring to some of the prophets, says, "It was revealed to them that they were serving not themselves but you, in the things which have now been announced to you by those who preached the good news to you through the Holy Spirit sent from heaven, things into which angels long to look." When Christians do the work of the household of God, there is an eternal crowd cheering them on from the grandstands (Heb. 12:1-2).

"He was preached among the nations."

The wonder of wonders is that the gospel is not just for a select group, the Jews, but has been made available for all people. This reflects the power behind the Great Commission: "Go therefore and make disciples of all nations" (Matt. 28:19-20).

The global gospel requires global concerns for the philosophy of ministry of every Christian congregation. Church growth is opening the eyes of Christians everywhere to see the billions of people who need to be reached with the gospel of Jesus Christ. The age of missions is not over. In many ways, it may be just beginning.

"He was believed on in the world."

When Christians give witness to Jesus Christ and his great acts of life, death, and resurrection, the world responds and believes. A church growth philosophy of ministry is not an attitude of pessimism and gloom. When we have faith, we trust in God for power to be the people of his household and fulfill the commission he has given.

"He was taken up in glory."

Jesus Christ is at the right hand of God. He is in the place of glory. He is in the place of power. He has promised the church that power. "But to all who received him, who believed in his name, he gave power to become children of God; who were born, not of blood nor of the will of the flesh nor of the will of man, but of God" (John 1:12-13). That's what the Incarnation is all about.

God's power comes in the flesh. That power touches people's lives, transforms them into the household of God, and puts power into their lives for the mission he has called them to carry out. These people are called *the church,* the community of those who acknowledge Jesus as Lord. This is the power that can change the world.

The Flock of God

A philosophy of ministry that is true to the biblical record will recognize the reality of the nature of humanity. The people of God are thought of as sheep. The psalmist declared, "The Lord is my shepherd; I have everything I need" (Ps. 23:1 TEV). A theological understanding of the church as a sheepfold requires the confession that we, like sheep, "have gone astray; we have turned every one to his own way" (Isa. 53:6)—we are sinners. Paul quoted Psalms to the Romans: "None is righteous, no, not one" (3:10; see also 3:23). That's bad news.

But the good news is that the Good Shepherd calls his people by name (John 10:3). Christians often have the idea that they can join the church. The Lord reminds people who chooses whom (John 15:16). The chief Shepherd is the Lord (I Peter 5:3-4). He is in charge. The people of the flock of Jesus Christ have been called by the Shepherd, who has lain down his life for his sheep (John 10:11, 15, 17; Heb. 13:20).

At the cost of his life, Jesus established himself as the door through which the sheep enter salvation. There is no other way (John 14:6; 10:20). The blood Jesus shed on the cross is the price he gave to obtain the sheep for himself. He is the one who guides and directs the flock, the one who will see that the sheep are safe and fed. Though he chooses servants to help feed and watch over the flock (Acts 20:28; I Peter 5:2), Christ is ultimately in charge (Col. 1:18).

Sometimes Christians fail to look to the Lord as the source of their strength. If the church is impotent in this world, the Lord is not to blame. The problem lies with those who will not accept his promise. The writer to the Hebrews declares that the great Shepherd, through the giving of his own blood, will equip God's people with everything they need to do his will (Heb. 13:20-21).

The Church Growth Movement points to the promises of the Lord and reminds the flock of the need to do great things for God. Robert Schuller says, "Nothing is more important than faith, and faith is believing it before you see it."[2] That faith is the confidence that God is at work in us (Phil. 2:13). The word *confidence* does not refer to puffed-up self-esteem, but comes from the Latin and means literally, *with faith*. Confidence in Christ is the faith that moves mountains (Matt. 17:20). Sheep do not have confidence in themselves or in other sheep. They have confidence in the Shepherd: "We have boldness and confidence of access through our faith in him" (Eph. 3:12).

The Good Shepherd is a great comfort to his sheep. They know he is leading them, but they also see in him their source of forgiveness and of life itself (I John 5:12). Jesus Christ is the redeemer. He has purchased forgiveness for the sheep. John the Baptist summarized the Shepherd's ministry, in which he took the place of his own sheep: "Behold, the Lamb of

God, who takes away the sin of the world!" (John 1:29).

The only people who can design a philosophy of ministry for growth are forgiven people. They do not witness what they are, but what they have become. No one is interested in the sheep, but everyone has an inner desire to meet the Shepherd. Christians do not boast of themselves, but of the Lord.

Many people criticize those who have a church growth-oriented philosophy of ministry. They call it a numbers game. Those people have not really studied church growth. No one will pay the price in time, energy, and money just for a chance to boast about membership statistics. God's call to ministry is in terms of responsibilities, not privileges (John 16:1-3; 21:18-19). From a church growth perspective, the Shepherd who knows all his sheep by name does not want even one to perish (II Peter 3:9; John 17:12).

It is precisely in relation to the flock that Jesus told the parable about the lost sheep. The shepherd left the ninety-nine to look for the one that had strayed (Matt. 18:12). Numbers? No. Sheep? No. People.

The Lord cares about people. He cares enough to count them, and he cares enough to go after the missing one. Church growth people follow their Lord's concern for the lost. "For the Son of man came to seek and to save the lost" (Luke 19:10).

A Royal Priesthood

A philosophy of ministry for church growth must be a doctrine that includes what the Reformers called the priesthood of all believers. Oscar Feucht maintains that this priesthood "is our greatest single hope for fulfilling God's mission."[3] A position in God's priesthood is not to be taken lightly, but is a tremendous privilege. Christians became a chosen race and a holy nation. They are God's own people (I Peter 2:9). The Greek text says they are "possessed" by God.

The church is God's community only because God makes it his own. It is distinguished from all other organizations by its unique relationship to him (Mal. 3:17), which he restored because he loved his people so much (Rev. 1:5; 5:10).

But God does not bring his people into that relationship so they can be delinquents. He did not shed the blood of his Son to organize a cult of pew sitters. He calls everyone to action. Every Christian is a priest of the royal priesthood. And it is a royal priesthood because Christ the King is the commanding priest.

One of the most strongly emphasized church growth principles is mobilization of the laity. Christianity began as a lay movement, and the enormous growth of the early church was due to lay people. Down through the centuries, Christianity became officialized—first by the decree of an emperor (Constantine of Rome) and then in the minds of the people.

The vast gap between clergy and laity has led to the sickening practice of the "sacrament of the seat"—observed by the masses of lay people stuck on their ecclesiastical backsides. The whole situation has paralyzed God's ingenious plan to multiply ministry and win the world.

Harvey is a good example of a paralyzed church member. He is a fine Christian with spiritual gifts that have been well developed for effective ministry. His Christian maturity is deep. He knows his Savior. He knows his Bible. Now Harvey is retired and truly desires to serve the Lord. But he is frustrated. All his life he has been told, implicitly and explicitly, that significant ministry can be accomplished only by the ordained clergy. He feels he is too old to go to seminary. For a church or denomination to require six to eight years as the *only* way a person can become a minister is one of the greatest deterrents to church growth.

God never intended that *all* his full-time servants must go to seminary for several years. The priesthood of all believers has more authority behind it than a college or seminary diploma. Every believer is called by God—not just to sit in the pew and pay the bills, but to "declare the wonderful deeds of him who called you out of darkness into his marvelous light" (I Peter 2:9).

John writes in Revelation that the Lamb has called his people "from every tribe . . . and nation" (5:9). The Lord's call is comprehensive. It calls people from *everywhere*. *Everyone* is to be a priest, to witness to *all people*. As a church begins to develop a philosophy of ministry toward church growth, it should remember the words of Isaiah (61:16; also see Exod. 19:16):

> You shall be called the priests of the LORD,
> Men shall speak of you as the ministers of our God.

The Bride of Christ

The prophet Hosea probably did not win any popularity contests among the Israelites of his day, simply because, as God had directed, he told Israel she was a harlot (Hos. 9:1). The unfaithfulness that characterized the people in Hosea's time was viewed by God as adultery. This is the graphic way God spoke of a relationship as intimate as that between husband and wife. In fact, the Hebrew word used to describe "knowing" God is the same terminology often used to describe sexual intercourse. The point is that God wants his people to see themselves in a constant intimate relationship with him.

A church that desires to develop a philosophy of ministry should be aware of the scriptural symbol of the people of God as the bride of Christ (Mark 2:18-22). The church is to be Christ's bride in purity and devotion. Concerned that the Corinthians were being led astray from sincere devotion to their Lord, Paul reminded them that they had been betrothed to Christ (II Cor. 11:2-3).

The Lordship of Jesus Christ is essential to healthy church growth. Faithfulness to the Bridegroom is part of the ongoing relationship with the Lord. Christians live in a state of grace; therefore forgiveness is part of their daily lives. Forgiveness and newness of life are gifts that cause God's people to respond in faithfulness and obedience.

Jesus' parable of the ten maidens (Matt. 25:6) is a lesson in eschatology—the last times. It reflects the importance of faithfulness as it relates to preparedness. Jesus, the Bridegroom, will one day return. He will come suddenly, and he wants his people to be ready. The oil for the lamps of the ten maidens is a symbol of fidelity and perseverence. This is an important lesson for the church if it wants to live as the bride of Christ.

Frequently, the church reflects a people who do not know their purpose and direction as the people of God in this world. The church is involved in extracurricular activities that take it away from its spiritual mission to the whole person in the whole world. Potlucks and picnics have their place, but too much introspection makes the bride of Christ a spiritual navel gazer. Meanwhile, some so-called church members have no assurance of eternal life, do not live a life of victory in the Lord, are biblically illiterate, and could not witness to their Lord if the opportunity came up and kicked them in their pious shins. The wise maidens in the parable had oil—fidelity and perseverence. To be "wise" in biblical terms is to have only one Bridegroom, one source of faith and hope. It is to look to God for all things (Eccl. 9:1).

Five maidens in Jesus' parable were foolish. They let their lamps go out. They didn't have enough oil (fidelity and perseverence). While they were shopping for more oil, the bridegroom returned. The wise maidens went into the marriage feast with him, and the door was shut. When the foolish maidens returned and tried to get in, the bridegroom responded in the same intimate, relational way. Like the symbolism used by the prophet Hosea, the bridegroom said, "I do not know you" (Matt. 25:12).

The bridegroom is the bride's first love. At the end times, according to the book of Revelation, there will be those who lose their first love (2:4-5). The church at Ephesus lost its first love. The angel warned that it would lose its lampstand—perhaps a reference to the destruction of that church. As the bride of Christ, the church must remain faithful to its Bridegroom.

A philosophy of ministry for a growing church is a declaration of an intimate love affair with the eternal Bridegroom.

The Body of Christ

The Church Growth Movement has made good use of the Body of Christ as a symbol. As we have seen, it is not the only biblical symbol of the nature of the church, but it provides some good insights for a congregation that desires to develop a thoroughly biblical philosophy of ministry.

"Body of Christ" defines the structure of the church as a living organism. Christ is the head; the believers are members of the body. Jesus Christ is in charge in the church, the source of all the body's functions (Eph. 1:22). The head of the church is an irreplaceable part; without it the body dies (Eph. 5:29).

On the other hand, a head, in order to function, needs a body. Christ directs his power in this world toward the expression of himself through his people, the church. This does not mean that Christ cannot act outside his body, but he channels his mission through the church. The church is "the fulness of him" (Eph. 1:23); a body that is to be responsive to the impulses of Christ, ready to carry out his purposes at whatever cost. And Christ's purpose is to grow to completeness. This means that the church is to grow *up* to maturity and *out* bodily (Eph. 4:16).

The Body of Christ is a unity—many parts, but one body (I Cor. 12:12, 20; Rom. 12:4-5; Eph. 4:16). When each part works properly, it is a healthy, growing body. This analogy is used in connection with the teaching on spiritual gifts (Eph. 4:11; I Cor. 12:4; Rom. 12:6). As in the analogy of the royal priesthood, the nature of the church as the Body of Christ signifies that every part has a function.

A Christian's job description as part of the Body of Christ is defined by his or her spiritual gifts, the supernatural attributes given by the Holy Spirit at the time a person becomes a Christian. The Church Growth Movement emphasizes that every Christian should be involved in the process of discovering, developing, and using these spiritual gifts.

A congregation that desires to develop a church growth philosophy of ministry must recognize the church as a body, with Christ at the head and each member as a part of that body. Furthermore, bodies are meant to grow. God expects growth. It is normal for God's church to grow. If it is not growing, it is because we are doing something to hinder God's desires.[4]

A Biblical Philosophy

A philosophy of ministry that reflects a church growth attitude must be thoroughly biblical. If it is biblical, it will be Christ-centered and growth-oriented. Jesus Christ established his church on earth to carry out his redemptive purposes. He desires to be in relationship with all the people. He is in control. He is the Good Shepherd. He is the Cornerstone and the Foundation. He is the Head of his Body. He has called out the priesthood. He has given the church a mission, a commission, a command, a challenge, a world. He has given it time and resources. What a church does with these challenges and blessings will greatly reflect its philosophy of ministry. There is no choice. A church's philosophy of ministry must reflect Christ's eternal purposes.

Discussion Questions for Chapter V

1. How would members of your congregation describe your church—as an institution, as a building, or as a living organism? List the ways your congregation could promote a more biblical understanding of the church.

____

____

____

____

2. How much training is required for a person to become a member of your church? Does this training include a proper understanding of the nature of the church?

___

___

___

3. Is the attitude of your membership toward the pastor one that reflects an understanding of the royal priesthood? If not, what steps would you take to promote a biblical understanding of what it means to be one of God's people?

___

___

___

___

4. Does your church train the people for ministry? Are boards and committees elected just to fill vacancies, or are people chosen and trained on the basis of their spiritual gifts, their Christian calling, and the challenge to make disciples of all nations? What changes could you suggest for mobilizing the lay people of your church for ministry?

___

___

___

5. Is the Lordship of Jesus Christ stressed at your church? Is discipleship the *stated* intention and goal for members of your church? Is it the *real* goal—as demonstrated by programs and activities? What improvements could you suggest?

VI

Putting a Philosophy of Ministry to Work

A philosophy of ministry serves the ultimate goal of church growth to the glory of Jesus Christ. Used in any other way, it is non-Christian. Congregations that use it to draw attention to themselves, to glorify the leadership, or to make a name for the pastor are misusing the philosophy. Abuse of a philosophy of ministry is not in harmony with the spirit of the Church Growth Movement.

John the Baptist summarized the Christian's proper perspective: "He must increase, but I must decrease" (John 3:30). Therefore a church's philosophy of ministry is never an end in itself, but a tool that can be used in several ways. It is a means to an end—the making of disciples.

Vision

A philosophy of ministry can set a vision before the people. Proverbs 29:18 says, "Where there is no vision, the people perish" (KJV). The Good News Bible translates, "A nation without God's guidance is a nation without order."

A philosophy of ministry is a tool. Its content will reflect the will of God as revealed to a particular group of people, at a certain place, at a specific moment in history. In this way, the philosophy serves as a banner to be held in front of God's people. It is a vision, a goal, a dream that fuels the fires of enthusiasm and sparks the creative imagination.

All too often the local church has no vision. Week after week, the congregation plods along doing business as usual. If ten different people are asked, "What is the vision for this church in the next decade?" ten different answers will emerge. This kind of schizophrenic view of purpose is not good for the Body of Christ. People need a vision.

God's people today are hungry for a vision. Several years ago Madalyn Murray O'Hair began to wage war against the United States Federal Communication Commission (FCC). She objected to Christian broadcasting. This was seen by Christians as a real threat to the use of radio and television for the spreading of the gospel. Suddenly Christians had a flag to wave, a banner to fly.

The FCC received thousands upon thousands of letters from Christians around the United States—so much mail that the government spent a tremendous amount of money just to open and sort it. Even after it was determined that the issue would not become a threat, letters continued to pour in. Denominations had to plead with their people not to send any more protests. The momentum was difficult to subdue, because Christian people had a cause. They had a vision.

Usually, a vision for a local church is set only when a new building program has been initiated and financial support is required. Many people testify to the special joy and excitement involved during a building program, planting a daughter congregation, or buying a new organ. The air is charged with anticipation. People are working together, praying and paying. There is a vision!

There is nothing wrong with having a temporary vision tied to a building program or a new organ. But there is no reason why an overall vision can't be established for a congregation. A philosophy of ministry can help to set that vision before the people. God's people need to rally around the banner of making disciples of all peoples.

Focus

Visiting the various boards, committees, and organizations of a church can be an interesting experience. In this church, for instance, the visits could be very confusing: The women's group has decided to hold a bazaar to raise money to resurface the parking lot. The trustees, who are in charge of physical details (such as the parking lot), have considered the lot's condition and felt it had a lower priority than painting the church. The trustees are therefore drawing up a proposal to ask the women of the church to sponsor a bazaar to raise money for paint. Meanwhile, the evangelism committee has seen the need for a bus ministry and is drawing up a request to buy a bus with money that could be raised by asking the women to sponsor a bazaar. The social ministries committee has just proposed a counseling ministry for unwed mothers, and they want the women's group to raise money for a professional counselor. On and on the suggestions go, until the church looks like an uncoordinated octopus that can't get its arms together to move in any one direction.

A philosophy of ministry will not remove the need to administer a multifacted ministry. It will not eliminate meetings of the governing board. Planning sessions still will be important, and goal setting still will be essential. Efforts to coordinate the Body of Christ still will be needed. But a *philosophy of ministry will help to develop a unified focus for programming and goal setting.*

People are often fuzzy about the overall direction of the congregation. Some people may see the church as a training center for Christian growth. Others see it as a harbor of peace in the rough seas of world problems, as the embodiment of One who said, "Come to me, all who labor and are heavy laden, and I will give you rest" (Matt. 11:28).

Still others may understand the church to be an agency for sending God's people into the world each week, reflecting the Lord's command to "go therefore and make disciples" (Matt.

28:19). When these people with various perspectives come together in a committee to make decisions and plan programs, nothing short of chaos can emerge.

When tensions exist among leadership groups in such a church, the action taken to resolve that tension may be directed at symptoms, rather than at the root cause. A better solution is for the whole congregation to hammer out a philosophy of ministry, adopt it, and follow it. The philosophy then provides a focus for the overall ministry of the church.

To borrow the analogy of baseball, church leaders, boards, committees, and organizations need not play the same position or even have the same skills (gifts). It takes many different kinds of people to make a good team. Not all are out on the field—there are trainers and coaches and managers and groundskeepers. All are important. With an accepted philosophy of ministry, at least everyone is in the same ballpark: They've all agreed to play the game!

Measurement

Every congregation that takes stewardship seriously should take an annual inventory. A financial inventory is usually taken in terms of income and payments. Sometimes churches inventory hymnbooks, choir robes, or Sunday school materials. But what about an inventory of the church's general direction and self-image?

A philosophy of ministry can be used as a tool for reflection and measurement. At regular intervals, the people of the church should evaluate their ministry to see whether they are following their intended overall goals. If the church has developed a philosophy of ministry strongly based on Christian education, what has been the response in the Sunday school over the past year? What were the opportunities for adults to grow in the Lord during that time? How many people were involved? Were more involved than the year before? What other programs have reflected that philosophy of ministry? How much time and energy have been invested toward the priorities set forth by the philosophy of ministry?

Churches frequently have good intentions about performing a certain area of ministry, but the reality may be greatly different. For example, Grace Church verbally professed a philosophy that emphasized the desire to meet the physical needs of the poor in the immediate community. Since that philosophy wasn't written, there was no measuring device to see whether that was *in fact* their priority ministry. When a philosophy of ministry is written, it can be used as a measurement of time and energy actually spent by the congregation.

When an annual inventory of ministry is conducted, a philosophy of ministry can be used as a measuring device also against budget disbursements. Money doesn't always reflect priorities, but it does tend to indicate what the congregation considers most important.

At Immanuel Church, the leadership faced the sobering exercise of taking inventory of their budget expenditures. The previous year, they had recognized that their community was in the process of racial change. They had declared themselves to be a mission congregation with cross-cultural ministry as the top priority. They developed a philosophy of ministry that was adopted by the congregation. One year later, when that philosophy was used as a reflective tool to evaluate the previous twelve months' expenditures, they discovered that the congregation had spent almost every penny on *itself*. When this fact was brought before the people of the church, they realized they were *in reality* survival-oriented, not outreach-oriented. This feeling was so strong that the philosophy of ministry was changed drastically. Eventually the church accepted the fact that it would one day die in that community, and it adopted a death-with-dignity philosophy. The inventory helped the congregation struggle through a very important stage in its history.

Communication

When new people enter a congregation, they must understand the church's philosophy of ministry. *A philosophy of ministry can help communicate the church's image to new members.*

New members come into a church in one of three ways: *Biological growth* is represented by church members' children who grow up and join the church; *transfer growth* comes about as Christians from other churches transfer into the congregation; *conversion growth* takes place when non-Christians are converted and join the church.[1]

Frequently, new members will have their own notions about the image of a church. If they differ in their philosophy, eventual conflict will result. Either they will sense something different from what they expected and will be disappointed and leave, or they will gather others of like mind and begin to work for change. The latter situation has developed into church splits, in some instances.

Recognizing the need to assimilate new members, many congregations hold series of classes. These are geared not only for theological teaching but also to help new members recognize the features that make a particular church different from the one down the road.[2] Another technique to help people see the image and nature of a particular church is an application for membership. This can reflect some tone of the church's nature and is often signed by those desiring membership. Sometimes the process includes a review of the application by the pastor, a board of elders, or some other governing board.

A personal interview with the pastor or an elder also can help new members become familiar with the philosophy of ministry of the congregation. The prospective members are told about the vision and priorities and are helped to catch the image of the church they are seeking to join. The use of a philosophy of ministry for assimilating new members is gaining wide acceptance among church growth-oriented congregations.

Publicity

A philosophy of ministry can be used to publicize the image and identity of the church. Most people who are not members of the church have little knowledge of the Christian church. They have even less knowledge about the particular identity of a local congregation. Furthermore, misconceptions about a church may actually hinder its mission.

Publicity aimed at the community is very important. A church need not use its philosophy of ministry in its actual form, but it can be very helpful for setting the tone for publicity. It also will help assure that publicity is accurate.

Some congregations have programs in which members regularly walk through the community. Volunteers knock on doors, give warm greetings to the people on behalf of the congregation, and invite them to visit the church. Frequently some type of literature is left at each home. Other congregations send out mass mailings of newsletters which detail activities and programs of the church. This literature may not contain a church's philosophy of ministry, but it should reflect it. Some congregations make extensive use of local newspapers, while some utilize radio and television.

Any form of publicity should be checked against the philosophy of ministry of the congregation. Does it truly reflect the image of the church? Does it clearly tell the priorities? Does it present an honest and realistic picture of the church? When people see the publicity and decide to attend the church, will they find what they expected? If they do, many will return a second and third time.

Staffing

Most congregations have only one pastor. But as churches grow and the ministry becomes more specialized, staff members are often added.

Church growth teaches that the pastor is the single most important factor for the growth of a congregation. The church staff also is very important, since it can be considered an extension of the pastor. Yet it is often reported that a certain person was hired but left the congregation after a few months because "things just didn't work out."

Behind the nebulous "things didn't work out" often is the reality that the new staff member felt he or she didn't "fit." This can reflect a conflict of philosophy of ministry. *A written philosophy of ministry can be of help when seeking new staff members.*

One pastor relates that for years his congregation had worked to establish a church growth philosophy of ministry. The philosophy was verbalized, accepted, and in the background of every plan and program. But it wasn't written. Furthermore, it wasn't used in obtaining new staff. Then came Jim and Martha.

Jim and Martha had been married for about a year. They had just finished college and were very enthusiastic about their first assignment as teachers in a Christian school. They were excited about joining a large staff of ministers, teachers, evangelists, counselors, and administrators. Many members of this staff had served the church for several years and had adapted to the church growth philosophy of ministry. The problem was that no one knew it.

When Jim and Martha were interviewed, the philosophy of ministry was never discussed. As months passed, conflict arose. The staff tried to deal with the symptoms, but no one really recognized the cause of tension. Finally the senior minister realized the radical differences in philosophy of ministry and the unwillingness of the young couple to accept the church's position. He called them into his office and presented their alternatives. They would need to either change their philosophy or seek to minister elsewhere. The next morning they both resigned.

How sad it is when congregations seeking staff members share everything but their own identity. They tell prospective members about salary, fringe benefits, and job descriptions. They usually relate information about the congregation and community. It would be helpful if they also would communicate the church's philosophy of ministry.

A Useful Tool

A philosophy of ministry is a useful tool for a congregation that wants to grow. It is not a goal in itself, but a guideline to help develop strategies to reach goals—a means to an end.

To be used properly, a philosophy must be written. It must be concrete. It must be accepted and owned by all the people of the church. Like any tool, it isn't much good unless it is used.

A philosophy of ministry is not a document written just to become lost in the minutes of meetings. It is a banner to be hoisted before the people again and again. It is a flag to be flown, a vision to be seen. It is a yardstick for sizing up the performance of the church. It is a visual aid for those who want to know more about the church, and it is a picture of true identity for those who want to become a part of God's people in a particular place. A philosophy of ministry is a tool to be used.

Discussion Questions for Chapter VI

1. Is there a general vision for the direction of your church? What do you think that is? Compare your answers. Does everyone in your discussion group share the same vision?

____

____

____

____

____

2. Does any group in your church annually review the programs and budget of the previous year and compare the results to the overall general direction of the congregation? If not, how could such a procedure be set up?

____

____

____

____

____

____

____

3. Make a chronological chart showing the year each person in your discussion group joined your church. Reflect on your perceptions of the church *before* you joined. Add each person's answers to the chart beside the proper year.

   Were there differences from year to year? Is there a trend of image change (a shifting philosophy of ministry) in your congregation? If so, were you aware of it?

____

____

____

____

____

4. In what concrete ways could the philosophy of ministry of your church be communicated to your community?

VII

How to Discover Your Church's Philosophy of Ministry

A congregation that desires to develop a church growth philosophy of ministry must begin by discovering the church's present philosophy. There probably is no formal draft, but it does exist! A philosophy of ministry is the accepted recognition of certain priorities that take precedence over others. There is a congregational identity expressed by the corporate body, whether on a conscious level or not.

In order to develop a church growth philosophy, a church must first raise its own identity to a level of consciousness. That identity must be discovered, formulated, and written out. It must be discussed, then accepted. It will then be the basis for moving toward an identity in tune with the Great Commission goal of "making disciples of all nations" (Matt. 28:19).

Discovering a congregation's identity is a task of introspection and diagnostic research while remaining as objective as possible. Clues might come from the constitution. Hints might be obtained from bulletins and newsletters. Sometimes congregations employ a church growth consulting firm to guide an objective analysis. But if the people of the congregation are willing to do the work, the analysis can be achieved. And the analysis must be done if a church wants to develop a good, sound church growth philosophy of ministry.

Diagnostic Questions

A number of questions can help a congregation discover its present identity. With the answers, a philosophy of ministry will emerge. Those answers may not be the same from various groups in the congregation. Young people may see things differently than do older people. The pioneers (those who first organized the church) may have a perspective vastly different from that of the homesteaders (those who arrived on the scene after the congregation was established). Those who live in the immediate neighborhood may have different priorities from those who commute from distances.

The variety of answers will reflect the need to solidify some priorities of purpose. Discussion and Bible study groups should be formed so that meaningful communication can develop. Discovering a philosophy of ministry is not a boring chore. It is an exciting process of learning for all involved. Everyone in the church should have the opportunity to respond to four basic diagnostic questions.

What Is This Church All About?

This is a general question which gives people the freedom to respond in any way they wish. It helps people reflect upon the identity of their church, and for many it will be a good exercise in self-analysis. It's surprising how many people respond with, "Well, let's see, I never thought about that."

People tend to take their church for granted. Worse yet, there is a tendency to take their membership in the church for granted. But when a decision goes against them, they protest. It is not wrong to disagree. Some disagreement serves as a challenge to stimulate thought. Many people cannot articulate *why* they disagree, frequently because they are operating from the perspective of a different philosophy of ministry.

To reflect upon "what the church is all about" is a healthy exercise for every member. Some people will express a theological point of view: "This church is God's people . . . ."

Others will choose a sociological perspective: "This church is a group of people who have come together . . . ." Still others will reflect from a philosophical standpoint: "Love—that's what this church is all about." In reality, the church may be a little of all these views—just seen from different angles. A church is a complex organism. In the final analysis, no full identity of the congregation will emerge from any one person's answers. The philosophy of ministry will be forged out of the corporate responses—not only to this question, but to several others as well.

What Are the Church's Priorities?

A *priority* is something that comes first, that takes precedence over something else. A priority may or may not be reflected by the amount of time, energy, and money spent, because some things cost less than others, require less energy, take less time. Nevertheless, those things may take priority.

A priority can be determined in terms of *emphasis*. It reflects a quality of *importance*. A priority is best determined in contrast to other options. For example, the youth group must plan a project for the month. It can choose only one project, but three have been suggested: clean the sanctuary carpet, paint the nursery, or trim the shrubs. Regardless of what factors go into the decision, the choice will reflect a priority.

When a question about the church's priorities is asked, the responses may not directly indicate a philosophy of ministry. For example, a priority listed as "Christian education" may reflect a philosophy that goes much deeper than simply education. A high regard for God's Word or an emphasis on nurture may be reflected. Or if "Christian education" means that the church puts a high priority on a bus ministry to bring non-Christians into contact with the gospel, the actual priority may be evangelism. The answers must be analyzed to discover whether they represent an end in themselves, or are only means to an end. The way to probe an answer is to ask, "Why would you say your church sees that as a priority?"

As with the first diagnostic question, this analysis will become meaningful only as a number of responses are gathered from various members and groups within the church. As priorities are recorded, certain patterns or categories will emerge again and again. These will begin to reflect the emphases of the congregation as a whole.

What Makes This Church Different?

This question is a little more specific than the first two. What makes this church unique? Why is it different from other churches in this area?

Although people do not often talk about what makes their congregation special to them, they are aware of it. Unfortunately, this awareness is verbalized only when people move. The pastor of Chapel of the Cross received a letter from a former member who had moved to another state. "Pastor, this new church is nice, but it is just not Chapel of the Cross. We miss Chapel of the Cross so much." If the pastor were to ask why the former members missed the church, something specific about why it is unique might be discovered.

Without a concrete philosophy of ministry, people do not consciously think through the uniqueness of their church. Perhaps this is one of the factors behind the move-without-transfer syndrome. Every church has a number of people who move to other communities but do not transfer their membership. Many of these people do not join another church. Sometimes they "shop around" in the new community but can't find a church they like. One problem is that, as they shop, they are wearing ecclesiastical blindfolds. They don't know what they are seeking. They have trouble expressing the uniqueness, the identity, the philosophy of ministry of their former church, of which they felt such a vital part.

What a real help it would be to our mobile society if each church had a copy of its philosophy of ministry for public inspection and each church member were philosophy-of-ministry wise. That kind of wisdom could help people recognize the uniqueness of their own congregation and help them look for a new church home when they move.

Every church has God's gift of diversity. To discover that particular type of identity is one more step toward discovering a church's philosophy of ministry.

How Would You Describe This Church to a New Neighbor?

Seventy to ninety percent of people who join a church do so because of a friend or relative. Whether or not congregational members witness to Christ, a lot of talk about the church takes place during the week. It happens on the job, at school, over the phone, and over the fence.

People generally describe their church in a way that reflects its philosophy of ministry as they perceive it. Some will mention the pastor. Others will discuss the programs. Some will talk about the people who make up the church. Looking past these forms of expression, one sees the identity of the church being expressed.

There is no doubt that some people give a wrong idea about their church when they talk with others. Sometimes a negative picture is given. This turns people off to the possibility of attending and leaves them wondering why the person with this attitude is a member at that church. Sometimes what people perceive about their church is totally wrong; it reflects personal conjecture rather than the reality of the situation. Then if the people with whom they share this personal opinion visit the church, they are confused and perhaps disillusioned. They try the church once and never return.

When a church has developed a philosophy of ministry, members are more prepared to speak about the church intelligently and accurately. They become more aware that every church isn't for everybody. They begin to sense that some people will respond to their church and others will reject it—not always on theological or spiritual grounds, but because of the philosophy of ministry. With a philosophy of ministry, people will be able to more effectively tell others what their church is all about.

Write It!

The process of discovering a congregation's philosophy of ministry can be a revealing exercise for all concerned. By using the four diagnostic questions, the philosophy of ministry can begin to be clearly articulated. The questions should be asked of three different groups: the pastor(s), the leaders, and the general membership.

The Pastor

The head pastor is a vital figure in establishing a church's identity. Pastors will frequently forge out a philosophy of ministry during the beginning years of their first assignment. However, sometimes when these pastors take on a new congregation in a different location, they import that same philosophy of ministry. Lack of flexibility causes them to try to continue to operate with the old philosophy in a new setting.

Conflict also occurs when pastors stay at the same church for a number of years but fail to take inventory, reassess the congregation, and make appropriate changes in their philosophy. They are not operating with a conscious philosophy of ministry on a conscious level, not seeing the Body of Christ as a living, constantly changing organism. Many new people have joined the church, bringing different, fresh, more objective and relevant ideas. They begin to sense a church identity different from the pastor's philosophy of ministry. The conflict is there, but without a written philosophy of ministry, no one is exactly sure of the origin of the conflict. The real point of difficulty is that such conflict can greatly hinder the growth of the church, as in the case of the Reverend John Dean.

The Reverend Dean was pastor of one of the largest churches in his denomination. An intelligent, gifted young man, he led an aggressive ministry in one of the fastest growing areas of a large metropolitan city.

John Dean was always a church growth-type person. He sensed God's challenge in the Great Commission and saw the value of church growth principles. When asked several years ago if he had a philosophy of ministry for his church, he clearly articulated a point-by-point philosophy that was dynamic, exciting, biblical, and relevant for his situation. But it wasn't written!

As time went on, the Reverend Dean saw the need for the church to move. There was a great opportunity to buy a choice piece of land, big enough to expand the ministry of the church and develop a wide range of outreach activities. Conflict emerged, however, when the move was proposed to the congregation. Not sure of the reason for the conflict, the pastor tried several avenues to lift the vision of the people, but the conflict only grew worse.

Eventually John Dean left the church, taking six families with him. He concluded his ministry by saying to the congregation, "Only in the past few months have I realized that my philosophy of ministry [a church growth outreach type] is different from and in conflict with the philosophy of ministry of this congregation."

It is very important that the pastor answer the four diagnostic questions separately from the leaders and the general membership, and before hearing any responses from the others. The pastor also may want to write a rough draft of a personal philosophy of ministry. This can be used for comparison when the responses are gathered from the leaders and other members. The same procedure can be followed with a rough draft of an application for membership.

The Leadership

The leadership of the congregation consists of all the elected officers, as well as the board and committee members. It also includes the leading opinion makers, some of whom may not be serving in an elected or official capacity at the time. A retreat setting could be used for answering the diagnostic questions. Or perhaps the questionnaires could be taken home and returned in a week.

Each board and committee could meet separately to discuss the results. As the members share responses, a consensus of major factors can be compiled by an appointed secretary. The end result will reflect the identity of the congregation, from the perspective of that group.

When each board and committee has completed the process, the whole leadership group should come together. The atmosphere should be relaxed, the process exploratory. A facilitator can gather the main points from each group and record these on a chalkboard or overhead projector. A leadership perspective of the church's philosophy of ministry will begin to surface.

The General Membership

Those who are worshiping members but do not act in any official capacity also will have an idea of the congregation's philosophy of ministry. Their opinions are very important, for in most churches they are the majority.

Perhaps the best way to facilitate the diagnostic process with the general membership is to conduct on-the-spot interviews as members come and go at worship. Sometimes it is better for outsiders to conduct the interviews. Members should be made aware that they may be interviewed and should be asked for their cooperation. This can be done through announcements during the services or in the bulletin.

The first question might be, "What do you think your pastor would say this church is all about?" phrased so that the original encounter is not personal. It must be remembered that the commitment of the general membership may not be as high as that of the leadership. Therefore the first question is indirect, but the answer will reflect the person's idea of what the pastor might say and, in that way, reflect the person's own idea of the congregation's identity. The questions that follow could include: What are the priorities of this church? (What is most important?) Why would you say each of these emphases is important? What makes this church different from others? How would you describe this church to a new neighbor who has just moved into the community?

Identity from the Outside

While members must be surveyed to discover the identity of a congregation, the image of the church as perceived by outsiders is of equal importance. How do they see the philosophy of ministry of the congregation?

Information from a nonmember survey can be compiled by categories. Then a summary can be constructed, noting especially those items that recur frequently. This should be compared with similar summaries from the general membership, the leadership, and the pastor. It may be very revealing for a congregation to discover that the image it desires to project may be vastly different from the identity perceived by outsiders.

A Beginning

Even when all this information is compiled, the congregation has not finished the exciting task of discovering its philosophy of ministry. Many people should be included in the process of molding and shaping the various bits of information into a definitive statement. The involvement of all the members will insure ownership and stimulate thinking about the identity of God's people in a particular place. The process of discovery, itself, will begin to raise the congregation's consciousness that it is unique and has a particular ministry to perform.

It is also helpful to isolate certain variables in the data collected. Are there significant differences of opinion among different age groups? If so, why? Do the various boards and committees differ greatly in their perception of the congregation? If so, why? Does length of membership significantly affect people's perspective on the congregation's philosophy of ministry? If so, why? Probing some of these questions could be helpful as the church seeks not only to discover its philosophy of ministry but prepares to use that philosophy for the benefit and effectiveness of the Lord's kingdom.

The solidified philosophy of ministry should be presented to all members for comment, for reaction, and for adoption. This process can unify objectives and kindle the vision of the church. As soon as the congregation accepts the philosophy of ministry, it should be put to use. A date should be established for future review of the philosophy, with time set aside for a thorough inventory of ministry.

The discovery of a congregation's *present* philosophy of ministry is still only the beginning. It is a good and necessary step in the right direction. But as Christians, we seek the will of the Lord that his church must grow. In response to Jesus Christ, the congregation can now go on to the next step: It can develop a church growth philosophy of ministry.

Discussion Questions for Chapter VII

1. How can your discussion group promote interest in discovering the philosophy of ministry of your congregation? Develop specific strategies.

____

____

____

____

____

____

2. How will you go about conducting the discovery process? In what time frames? Develop specific strategies.

3. Who will be in charge? Who will be accountable to see that the process takes place?

4. What is the goal for the date of completion?

5. In what ways will you begin to build ownership of the end product by a wide range of people? This is an important factor.

6. How will the final results be communicated to every member of the congregation? How will the philosophy be adapted and adopted?

7. Who will be responsible to see that the philosophy of ministry is *used*? Who will take the suggestions in Chapter 6 and work them out for *your* situation? When and how will this be done?

VIII

Developing a Church Growth Philosophy of Ministry

A congregation that has discovered and articulated a philosophy of ministry can now take the next step: It can intentionally direct its philosophy of ministry toward church growth. Each congregation will have a different philosophy of ministry, but the tone and flavor will reflect good, sound church growth thinking. The end result is qualitative growth, as its members mature (Eph. 4:16), and quantitative growth, as the church reaches out (Acts 1:8).

A church growth philosophy of ministry cannot be simply written by the pastor or by a few leaders and then presented to the group. One pastor, feeling the urgency of his congregation's ministry, formulated a church growth philosophy, only to have it flatly refused when presented to the governing board.

While it certainly takes more effort and time to follow the group process, the end result is usually positive. In some congregations the process could conceivably take several years. Members need to be taught what God says about the church. The congregation needs to refocus on the will of the Lord for his people.

Word and Prayer

The best way to begin is with prayer and Bible study. Church growth is biblical, based on principles from God's Word. The

Bible is not a "how to" book of step-by-step methods for church growth. Such a simplistic misuse of Scripture is to be avoided. The Bible may not supply programs, but it does supply principles and these principles must be taught to God's people.

Today many organizations provide good Bible studies as well as regional workshops and seminars in church growth.[1] A number of excellent resources are available for use in Bible classes, discussion groups, workshops, and seminars.[2]

For a Christian to become a church growth person and for a church to become a church growth congregation, the *spiritual* perspective must be recognized and accepted. Some critics, perhaps ignorant of its teaching, think that church growth consists of a little Madison Avenue advertising with some fancy gimmicks. That's not true, as anyone who has studied it can relate.

Church growth is a theological conviction about what God wants his people to do in this world. It is not just an academic exercise or a confession of doctrine. It is a way of ministry, a way of life, and it all begins with a personal recommitment to the Lordship of Jesus Christ. It is a real test of trust and reliance to "take up the cross and follow him" (Matt. 16:24), to face the challenges and risks involved in church growth.

There is hard work ahead for a congregation that seriously attempts to carry out the New Testament commission to make disciples of the whole world. It costs money. It takes effort. It may cause divisions and dissensions. Jesus promised no easy road for those who would take his gospel to the world (Mark 13:9-13). The ministry of the apostles should be sufficient testimony that the way toward evangelization of the world is not the easiest route to travel.

Yet the joy of all heaven over one sinner who repents is a joy also felt by those who bring the good news to a dying world. Jesus endured the cross for the joy that was on the other side (Luke 15:10; Heb. 12:2). The journey leading to church growth begins in prayer. The congregation must be prepared for a spiritual change—a change with repercussions that will permeate the very core and fiber of every program and organization of the church.

Discover the Goal

A church growth philosophy of ministry must include the biblical goal of evangelism. Various churches describe this goal in different ways.

Lakeside Chapel is an inner-city congregation well known for its programs to meet people's needs. Its aggressive pastor is involved in city politics. The church is always busy with activities; the pastor often boasts that the lights of the church never go out. Sewing classes, woodworking clinics, and first-aid courses bring people from all over the community. When asked about evangelism, the pastor says, "*This* is our evangelism. We are God's people, present in the city. We have not moved to the suburbs like so many other churches. We are here. We love our neighbor. The people of this community will get the message of God's love by our actions."

Bellview Church is slightly different. Bellview also is a congregation with a variety of activities. A youth program centers around the gymnasium and music center. Senior citizens meet regularly and receive meals. A professional counseling service is available for people with problems. But Bellview is interested in much more than just being present in the world. Its evangelism includes presence, but it goes on to include proclamation. As one member puts it, "We plant the seed. We tell the good news of Jesus Christ. We spread the gospel and leave the results to God. When a person is told about Christ, that person is evangelized."

The Church of the Open Door is somewhat different from either of those churches. Its programs include a twenty-four-hour telephone hot line available for people in time of crisis, or when they are lonely and just want to talk. An extensive program is carried out in area nursing homes, providing elderly people with regular visits. A home for runaways is completely supported and professionally staffed by the Open Door. The church is present with people in their needs, and, like Bellview, the Open Door proclaims Jesus Christ as Savior and Lord. It is very much involved in sowing the seed. But as one leader explains, the church is concerned also that people become responsible members of the Body of Christ: "We are present. We proclaim the good news. But we don't call a person 'evangelized' until he or she has been persuaded by God to become a disciple. The Lord said we should go into the harvest. He is not interested in sowing without reaping. He wants people harvested into his kingdom."

The Great Commission helps to define the goal of evangelism. The Lord says, "Go therefore and make disciples of all nations, baptizing them in the name of the Father and of the Son and of the Holy Spirit, teaching them to observe all that I have commanded you" (Matt. 28:19-20). There are four relevant verbs in this section:

1. go
2. make disciples
3. baptizing
4. teaching

In the original Greek, one of these verbs is imperative and the others are participles. The imperative relates to the goal of the Great Commission—the end. The participles reveal the means to that end. The goal of the Great Commission is to *make disciples*. How do we make disciples? By going, baptizing, and teaching (see Figure 6).

The Verbs of the Great Commission

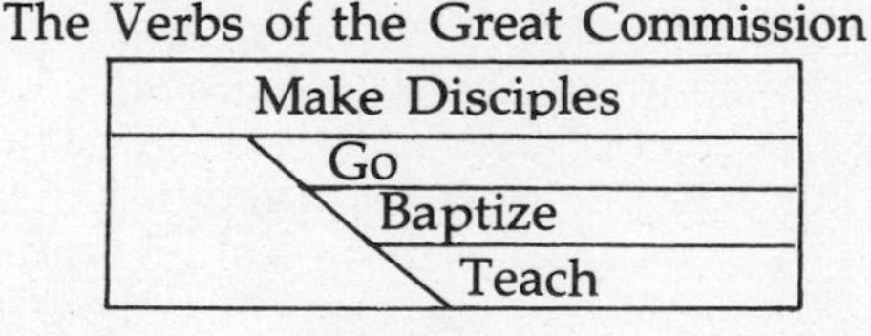

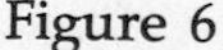
Figure 6

A church that bases its philosophy of ministry on the goal of making disciples is involved in persuasion evangelism. Such a church does not consider the task of evangelism completed until a person is persuaded by God to become a regular, active, responsible member of the congregation.

In church growth terminology, *presence, proclamation,* and *persuasion* evangelism are designated by these symbols: 1—P, 2—P, and 3—P (see Figure 7). A person can't be persuaded to be a disciple unless there is proclamation. A church can't proclaim unless it is present. As Paul points out in Romans 10:14-15, "How are men to call upon him in whom they have not believed? And how are they to believe in him of whom they have never heard? And how are they to hear without a preacher? And how can men preach unless they are sent?"

Presence, Proclamation, Persuasion Evangelism

1—P Presence	2—P Proclamation	3—P Persuasion
Lakeside Chapel	Bellview Community Church	Open Door Church

Figure 7

The formula for making disciples can be written as follows:

1—P + 2—P + 3—P = DISCIPLES

The goal of evangelism, the goal that reflects the purpose of the church, is the making of disciples. This is the goal that will be characteristic of a church growth philosophy of ministry. Unlike some evangelistic programs, which are interested only in numbers, church growth adds a qualitative dimension by emphasizing this goal of the Great Commission.

It is not enough to just plant the seed or just bring people into the church, for the goal of discipleship, *responsible* church membership, demands a maturing process. It puts the emphasis on nurture—sanctification, from the cradle to the grave. A church growth philosophy of ministry is developed on the basis of 3—P evangelism, the purpose of the church.

Discover the Gifts

A church growth philosophy of ministry is shaped around the gift mix of the congregation. As part of persuasion evangelism, church members will mature to the point that they can begin to discover their spiritual gifts.

There are three key biblical passages concerning spiritual gifts: Romans 12, First Corinthians 12, and Ephesians 4. In each, the analogy of the Body of Christ is used to describe the church. Christ is the head; the members of the body are the people of the church. Each person has an important function based on his or her gifts. These gifts are given to Christians when they enter the Body of Christ, and each person must discover his or her own so that they can be developed for use in the body.

If the members of the Body of Christ do not know their gifts, they may not know God's plan for the way they should function. Using the analogy of the human body, if a liver tried to function as a lung, it obviously would be doomed to failure. While that may sound absurd, if the members of a congregation do not know their gifts, many people may be misfunctioning. By discovering these spiritual gifts, a congregation can operate efficiently according to God's design.

Jim is a good example of the way gift discovery helps a Christian function properly. Jim had been a member of the church for many years. He sang in the choir for a while and then became a member of the board of directors, but neither role was very fulfilling. Frankly, his opinions were too negative to be of much help to the board. His good attitude toward the Lord and toward his church was not communicated well in that context.

Then Jim took part in a spiritual gifts workshop. He discovered he had the gifts of giving and hospitality, and he began to intentionally develop those gifts. Now he serves the church by opening his home to guests and by entertaining members of the congregation. With his gift of giving, he supports the Lord's work in his local church and also elsewhere in the world. Knowing and using his gifts, he is more efficient and more joyful in the Body of Christ.

When all members function according to their gifts, the church grows and "upbuilds itself in love" (Eph. 4:16). A church growth philosophy of ministry will be sensitive to spiritual gifts in two ways. First, the identity of the congregation will be based on the gift mix of the pastor, the leaders, and the general membership. This will help shape and mold the philosophy of ministry. Second, provision for the ongoing discovery of new members' gifts will be a vital part of any church growth philosophy of ministry. It is a common characteristic of healthy, growing churches that members know and use their gifts within the context of the Body.

Discover the Needs

When the church meets people's felt needs, the gospel is shared in a relevant way. A church growth philosophy of ministry is developed around those needs that the church can meet. Very rarely do people first attend a church because they are aware of a spiritual need. They usually come because of a *symptom* of a spiritual need. The symptom may be loneliness, a marital problem, or the desire to belong to a group. These are real needs which the church can meet. They serve as channels through which the gospel heals for the present and for eternity. A church growth philosophy of ministry is developed around the felt needs of two groups: (1) the people of the congregation and (2) others in the community who can be won for Christ.

While a congregation is developing a church growth philosophy, it must not be insensitive to the current members; therefore it is essential to involve a great number of people in the process. It is impossible for most congregations to be everything to everybody, in the sense that every felt need can be met. Since the average church is too small for that kind of comprehensive program, a philosophy of ministry will never be 100 percent effective for all the people all the time. It is based, rather, on the consensus of the majority of the people, meeting some of their needs—those that can be met within the limited resources of the congregation.

When a philosophy of ministry wrestles with which felt needs can be met, some people may leave the church. Some individuals, families, or whole groups may go elsewhere. Is this healthy church growth? In a positive way, yes. Those people either would have remained unhappy in their present church or would have left eventually because their needs were not being met. When people go elsewhere and find their needs met by a church with a philosophy of ministry that better fits them, they are healthier Christians, and the Church (both their former church and their new congregation) is better for it.

Peace Church is well known for its Christmas choral concerts. Throughout its fifty-year history, people had come for miles and filled the sanctuary to overflowing. Twenty years ago up to three thousand people would attend. Recently, however, the crowd began to decline drastically, and attendance is now down to fewer than one hundred, but the congregation still perpetuates the concert. Valuable time, energy, and money are poured into a ministry that no longer meets most people's needs. The church is notorious for its persistent refusal to face reality. Discovering the felt needs of its people will help a church shape a meaningful philosophy of ministry for the qualitative, inward and upward (maturing), growth of God's people.

For outward, quantitative growth, a church growth philosophy will be sensitive to the felt needs of the people of the community. A church cannot meet the felt needs of everyone; some people will have needs that are not common. That doesn't mean, however, that any person's needs are unimportant. People will be referred to other churches that can meet their particular needs. Since some needs are too great for a church's resources, a church growth philosophy of ministry also will include referral to government agencies or community organizations.

How does a congregation discover the felt needs of others in the community? Ask them! A rather simple survey can be taken by volunteers who go from door to door, asking a few short, basic questions. How could the church help you? What programs or services could our church sponsor that would be beneficial to you and/or your family? The answers will help the church get a "feel" for the community. A church growth philosophy of ministry will identify with the felt needs of those the congregation is trying to reach.

Think Conservative

Sociologist Dean Kelley writes that while many mainline denominations have declined, others, the more conservative denominations, have grown rapidly.[3] The word *conservative* does not necessarily mean just theologically conservative, but also includes those churches which stress that the purpose of the church is to provide meaning for life.

Seen from a theological point of view, the churches that are growing are those that emphasize the spiritual, supernatural, God-centered meanings, rather than peripheral matters. For example, meeting felt needs is not an end in itself, but a means to an end, a channel through which the gospel touches a person both for this life and for eternity.

Growing churches have been characterized as those that demand a lot from their members—one reason many sects have grown so rapidly. People are looking for a group of believers with integrity; they show interest in churches with backbone.

The Body of Christ does have a backbone. Jesus calls people to discipleship and obedience. He is demanding of his followers. The church always has been a gathering of those committed to the will of Jesus Christ. It is precisely at this point that many Christians feel uncomfortable with a philosophy of ministry. It is reasoned that a philosophy of ministry that makes demands on new members will turn people off. "You can't ask too much of people," some say. Just as a little child, deep down, desires discipline, so does the child of God. It is no mistake that the words *discipline* and *disciple* are so closely related.

A church growth philosophy will be biblically based and very articulate about what is expected of church members. A philosophy of ministry is not a new law, but a goal—a guideline and measurement for the personal discipline of God's people.

The church lives in grace. Members rejoice in the forgiveness won by Jesus Christ. As people freed by a new life in Christ, God's people desire to identify with one another in integrity and honesty. They declare their commitment to the Head of the church in word and in life. A church growth philosophy of ministry will both declare their intentions and guide their life together in the congregation.

Think Mission

What is mission? The dictionary defines *mission* as *an act or instance of sending*. In the various definitions, the common denominator can be summed up by *send*. Biblically, the meaning is the same. To think mission is to think outreach, to think beyond one's own little setting, to look outward to others. Christian mission is that God-given assignment to reach people with the gospel. It includes inreach for strength and outreach for expansion.

Too often the church dwells on maintenance. A church growth philosophy will point the church to growth on all levels. To establish this perspective, a philosophy of ministry should have a comprehensive view of evangelism. With the goal of making disciples, evangelism takes four different forms.

Internal growth is evangelism within the congregation. Every church has nominal members who are on the rolls but have not received Jesus Christ as their personal Savior. Almost every congregation has delinquent members who are inactive, lost, fallen away. Internal growth targets these two groups. It is evangelism designated by the church growth symbol E—O, and it takes place among church members. A church growth philosophy of ministry will assure that this happens.

Expansion growth, or E—1 evangelism, reaches out to non-Christians to win them for Christ and fold them into the Shepherd's flock. A church growth philosophy of ministry will include this type of outreach, which results in quantitative growth.

An emphasis on expansion will turn the attention of the congregation beyond its own boundaries to those with whom they come in contact during the week. Expansion growth will sensitize members to seek out those who do not know Christ and witness to them. It will challenge all members to be trained to effectively present the gospel to an unbeliever. It will direct those with the gift of evangelism to invest their time and energy in structured programs of witnessing.

Extension growth, also designated E—1, is outreach designed to establish new churches. In this type of evangelism, a congregation reaches out to people of a basically similar culture. Church planting can be one of the fastest ways to increase the kingdom of God.

A church growth philosophy of ministry will challenge church members to look for a place where God is opening up a ripe field, an opportunity to give birth to a daughter congregation. The joy, excitement, and health that result from starting a new church are well documented around the world.

Bridging growth takes place when churches are planted in a new culture. When the culture is not extremely different from that of the parent church, this is called E—2 evangelism. When it is greatly different, it is designated as E—3.

People become Christians more readily when they can do so within their own culture. This teaching, the *homogeneous unit principle,* has helped congregations see the need for E—2 and E—3 evangelism. A church growth philosophy of ministry shows sensitivity to the cultural mosaic in which we live, winning people to Christ by planting churches within their own culture.

Think Global

Jesus said, "You shall be my witnesses in Jerusalem and in all Judea and Samaria and to the end of the earth" (Acts 1:8). A church growth philosophy of ministry will begin in a church's own backyard. It will challenge members who have the gift to be missionaries to consider cross-cultural ministry. It will set a global vision by placing the congregation in the perspective of partnership with Christians around the world, working together for world evangelization.

A church growth philosophy of ministry will place a burden upon the hearts and lives of all members of the congregation. That burden will be the realization that billions of people in the world have yet to hear about Jesus Christ. It will touch people's lives through their prayers, efforts, and money. The philosophy of ministry will set the tone, challenge the commitment, and raise the vision of the commission of the King: "Go therefore and make disciples of all nations."

Discussion Questions for Chapter VIII

1. On a scale from 1 to 10, how would you rate the church growth attitude (theological conviction) among a significant number of people in your church?

____

____

2. Based on your answer to Question 1, what would you choose as a *realistic* time frame for developing a church growth philosophy of ministry for your congretation?

____

____

3. Based on your answers to Questions 1 and 2, what general step-by-step strategy would you suggest for achieving this goal within the chosen time frame?

4. When will you begin this process? What is the first step? (Be specific.) Who will take that first step and be responsible for it? Who will evaluate the effectiveness as the strategy continues? How will "success" be measured?

5. What resources can you list for the accomplishment of this task? Include the Lord's guidance, prayer, the power of the Spirit, and Scripture. What else? What people? Which books from the Bibliography? Which resource experts in the field of church growth? Which resource people from the congregation, the denomination, other church bodies?

Notes

II. What Is Your Philosophy of Ministry?

1. C. Peter Wagner, *Your Church Can Be Healthy* (Nashville: Abingdon Press, 1979), pp. 77-87.
2. Donald A. McGavran and Win Arn, *How to Grow a Church.* © Copyright 1973, Regal Books, Ventura, CA 93006, pp. 89-97. Fig. 3 on p. 28 is used by permission.
3. Donald Abdon, *Organizing Around the Great Commission* (Indianapolis: Parish Leadership Seminars, 1977), deals with the church constitution in depth.

III. The Origin of Identity

1. C. Peter Wagner, *Your Church Can Grow: Seven Vital Signs of a Healthy Church* (Glendale: Regal Books, 1976), p. 55.
2. Lyle E. Schaller, *Hey, That's Our Church!* (Nashville: Abingdon Press, 1975), pp. 93-94.
3. Robert H. Schuller, *Your Church Has Real Possibilities!* (Glendale: Regal Books, 1974), p. 137.

IV. A Theology for Establishing a Philosophy of Ministry

1. George W. Peters, *A Biblical Theology of Missions* (Chicago: Moody Press, 1972), p. 22.
2. Ibid., pp. 21-31.

V. New Testament Images for a Biblical Philosophy of Ministry

1. See Kent R. Hunter, *Six Faces of the Christian Church: How to Light a Fire in a Lukewarm Church* (Corunna, Ind.: Church Growth Analysis and Learning Center, 1983).
2. Robert H. Schuller, *Your Church Has Real Possibilities!* (Glendale: Regal Books, 1974), p. 6.
3. Oscar E. Feucht, *Everyone a Minister* (St. Louis: Concordia Publishing House, 1974), p. 143.
4. See Hollis L. Green, *Why Churches Die* (Minneapolis: Bethany Fellowship, 1972), p. 7.

VI. Putting a Philosophy of Ministry to Work

1. See Kent R. Hunter, *Foundations for Church Growth* (New Haven, Mo.: Leader Publishing Co., 1983), pp. 85ff.
2. See Lyle E. Schaller, *Assimilating New Members* (Nashville: Abingdon Press, 1978), pp. 73-75.

VIII. Developing a Church Growth Philosophy of Ministry

1. Three organizations serving in this area are:

   Church Growth Analysis and Learning Center
   Corunna, IN 46730

   Charles E. Fuller Institute of Evangelism and Church Growth
   Box 989
   Pasadena, CA 91102

   Institute for American Church Growth
   709 East Colorado Blvd., Suite 150
   Pasadena, CA 91101

2. A selected bibliography appears at the end of this book.

3. Dean M. Kelley, *Why Conservative Churches Are Growing* (New York: Harper & Row, 1972), pp. 1-6, 21-34, 47-55.

Selected Bibliography

Barber, Diane, and Hunter, Kent R. *Facing the Facts for Church Growth!* Corunna, Ind.: Church Growth Analysis and Learning Center, 1982.

Belew, M. Wendell. *Churches and How They Grow.* Nashville: Broadman Press, 1971.

Chaney, Charles L., and Lewis, Ron S. *Design for Church Growth.* Nashville: Broadman Press, 1977.

Cho, Paul Y. *More Than Numbers.* Waco, Tex.: Word Books, 1984.

Feucht, Oscar E. *Everyone a Minister: A Guide to Churchmanship for Laity and Clergy.* St. Louis: Concordia Publishing House, 1974.

Flynn, Leslie B. *Nineteen Gifts of the Spirit.* Wheaton, Ill.: Victor Books, 1974.

Gerber, Vergil. *God's Way to Keep a Church Going and Growing: A Manual for Evangelism/Church Growth.* Glendale: Regal Books, 1973.

Hunter, George. *The Contagious Congregation: Frontiers in Evangelism and Church Growth.* Nashville, Abingdon Press, 1979.

Hunter, Kent R. *Foundations for Church Growth.* New Haven, Mo.: Leader Publishing Co., 1983.

———. *Gifted for Growth: An Implementation Guide for Mobilizing the Laity*. Corunna, Ind.: Church Growth Analysis and Learning Center, 1983.

———. *Launching Growth in the Local Congregation: A Workbook for Focusing Church Growth Eyes*. Corunna, Ind.: Church Growth Analysis and Learning Center, 1981.

———. *Six Faces of the Christian Church: How to Light a Fire in a Lukewarm Church*. Corunna, Ind.: Church Growth Analysis and Learning Center, 1983.

———. *Your Church Has Doors: How to Open the Front and Close the Back*. Corunna, Ind.: Church Growth Analysis and Learning Center, 1982.

Kelley, Dean M. *Why Conservative Churches Are Growing*. New York: Harper & Row, 1972.

Ladd, George Eldon. *The Gospel of the Kingdom*. Grand Rapids: William B. Eerdmans Publishing Co., 1959.

Lawson, E. LeRoy, and Yamamori, Tetsunao. *Church Growth: Everybody's Business*. Cincinnati: Standard Publishing Co., 1975.

McGavran, Donald A. *Understanding Church Growth*. Fully Revised. Grand Rapids: William B. Eerdmans Publishing Co., 1980.

McGavran, Donald A., and Arn, Winfield C. *Ten Steps for Church Growth*. San Francisco: Harper & Row, 1977.

Orjala, Paul R. *Get Ready to Grow*. Kansas City, Mo.: Beacon Hill Press, 1978.

Schaller, Lyle E. *Assimilating New Members*. Nashville: Abingdon Press, 1978.

———. *Growing Plans*. Nashville: Abingdon Press, 1983.

———. *The Multiple Staff and the Larger Church*. Nashville: Abingdon Press, 1980.

Schuller, Robert H. *Your Church Has Real Possibilities*. Glendale: Regal Books, 1974.

Tippett, Alan R. *Church Growth and the Word of God: The Biblical Basis of the Church Growth Viewpoint*. Grand Rapids: William B. Eerdmans Publishing Co., 1970.

Wagner, C. Peter. *Leading Your Church to Growth: The Secret of Pastor/People Partnership in Dynamic Church Growth*. Ventura, Calif.: Regal Books, 1984.

———. *On the Crest of the Wave: Becoming a World Christian*. Ventura, Calif.: Regal Books, 1983.

———. *Your Church Can Grow: Seven Vital Signs of a Healthy Church*. Glendale: Regal Books, 1976.

———. *Your Spiritual Gifts Can Help Your Church Grow*. Glendale: Regal Books, 1979.

Werning, Waldo J. *Christian Stewards: Confronted and Committed*. St. Louis: Concordia Publishing House, 1982.

———. *Vision and Strategy for Church Growth*. Second Edition. Grand Rapids: Baker Book House, 1977.

Yamamori, Tetsunao, and Lawson, E. LeRoy. *Introducing Church Growth: A Textbook in Missions*. Cincinnati: Standard Publishing Co., 1975.